From a Parish Base

From a Parish Base

Essays in Moral and Pastoral Theology

KEVIN T. KELLY

DARTON · LONGMAN + TODD

First published in 1999 by
Darton, Longman and Todd Ltd
1 Spencer Court
140–142 Wandsworth High Street
London SW18 4JJ

ISBN 0–232–52315–0

A catalogue record for this book is available from the British Library.

Designed and produced by Sandie Boccacci
using QuarkXPress on an Apple PowerMac
Set in 9 1/4/13pt Stone Serif

Printed and bound in Great Britain by
Redwood Books, Trowbridge, Wiltshire

Contents

Introduction

While not denying the need for academic theology and Church law, I have in recent years seen my particular vocation as one of fusing together the experience and concerns of a professional moral theologian and a priest engaged in parish ministry. My very enriching pastoral experience as leader of a team ministry in Skelmersdale New Town was able to feed on and interact with my previous five years at Upholland Northern Institute. Together with lay-people and priests, I was engaged in exploring what moral theology according to the mind of Vatican II should mean for the problems of everyday life and pastoral ministry in the parish. During the years I was the lecturer in moral theology at Heythrop College in the University of London, I was also deeply immersed in pastoral ministry in a parish in inner-city Liverpool. When I was invited to teach Christian Ethics and later become part-time Senior Research Fellow in Moral Theology at Liverpool Hope University College, I continued my pastoral ministry in Our Lady's, Eldon Street. Having recently become parish priest in an exciting ecumenical venture at St Basil and All Saints, Hough Green, Widnes, my professional involvement in moral theology at Liverpool Hope consists at present in writing and giving occasional lectures.

Consequently, since 1975 I have been working on the interface between theological reflection and practical experience. I have grown more and more convinced that the experience of ordinary people in their everyday lives must be taken seriously since it is an important and challenging resource for theological reflection. As Jack Mahoney puts it, a moral theologian is engaged in 'trying to make faith-sense of experience and at the same time of making experience-sense of faith'.[1]

Even today for many people the main experience of Church, for better or for worse, occurs in the parish to which they belong, whether their belonging is territorially based or not. Experience-based theological reflection on the life and mission of a parish remains, therefore, high on the agenda for pastoral theology. That is why I decided to make the parish and parish-based ministry the main focus of Part 1 of this book.

Chapter 1 offers a blueprint for a parish which wants to build on the vision of Vatican II while responding to the needs of a world and Church which has changed considerably since the heady days of that Council. This chapter was originally written as a tribute to Archbishop Derek Worlock's commitment to the Council's vision of church throughout his years in Liverpool during a period of great social upheaval and rapid change. The chapter does not limit itself to the actual thinking and practice of Derek Worlock but pushes beyond it. I certainly would not want to claim that, were he alive today, the Archbishop would approve of every item on the parish agenda which I put forward. However, I believe that the whole agenda is true to his spirit. That is why I do not hesitate to link his name with the kind of parish I outline. Quite a few parishes have told me that they have used the material in this chapter as a kind of audit to help them monitor their commitment to continuing the renewal process set in motion at Vatican II. By making this chapter more widely available my hope is that more parishes will be able to use it as a tool for pastoral appraisal. Most parishes will recognise themselves in many of the characteristics mentioned. In that way I hope it will be a source of encouragement to them. Other characteristics might be more challenging and open out new avenues to the future. Like all of us as individual persons, every parish needs to continue growing and developing. Having just moved to a different parish myself, I am hoping that the criteria suggested in this chapter will provide a helpful self-appraisal exercise for the Roman Catholic and Anglican communities involved in our shared church. My initial impression is that the shared life and ministry of our two parish communities are very much in line with the criteria proposed. That is the fruit of the vision, commitment and painstaking hard work of parishioners and clergy over the past fifteen or so years since the parish was first founded. If I am true to my conviction about the importance of learning from experience, I suspect that I may well want to change or add to what I have written in the light of what I will be learning through living in my new situation. That will also be true of each reader of this chapter. From your own experience you will certainly be able to enrich further what is written in these pages.

Chapter 2 also takes Liverpool as its starting point. The undeniable phenomenon of parishes being affected by a steady decline in church attendance was particularly evident in the area of inner-city Liverpool where I was engaged in parish ministry for many years. Admittedly, this decline was due partly to the movement of population away from the area during the early days of post-war city regeneration. In this chapter I tell the remarkable story of the Eldonian community in the Vauxhall area of inner-city Liverpool and I reflect on my experience as a priest in the local parish of Our Lady's, Eldon Street. When I stand back and reread this chapter, I discover that I am doing exactly what Jack Mahoney referred to in the passage quoted earlier. I am 'trying to make faith-sense of experience and at the same time making experience-sense of faith.' Although the spotlight in this chapter is on the very local situation of the Eldonian community, its pastoral relevance is much more universal. I know that is true from the appreciative response I have invariably received when, over the years, I have shared the fruits of this very formative pastoral experience with people from other parts of the British Isles and beyond who made up the rich variety of mature students on the Pastoral Diploma course at Heythrop College in the University of London. As a postscript to this chapter I have added most of the text of a long letter I wrote to my archbishop, Patrick Kelly, as I was leaving Our Lady's. It explores a number of fundamental questions linked to parish reorganisation in the inner city, including such key issues as the processes of consultation and decision-making involved and the relationship between church buildings and a living parish community.

Chapter 3 was written while I was leader of the Skelmersdale

Team Ministry during the years 1980 and 1985. At that time, the team ministry was a very imaginative and exciting initiative in collaborative ministry. When I joined it in 1980 it had already been in operation for a number of years. The priests, religious sisters and laity involved in the main leadership group had invested a lot of time and effort in getting professional help to train them in the skills necessary for collaborative ministry. Archbishop Worlock and the archdiocesan authorities had demonstrated their commitment to this innovative type of ministry by creating a new form of parish structure which would make it possible. When Skelmersdale New Town was established (incorporating the older Lancashire village of Skelmersdale), instead of establishing the three or four traditional parishes needed to cater for the town's estimated Catholic population, Archbishop Worlock decided that the whole of Skelmersdale should form just one parish. It would be made up of seven smaller eucharistic communities, corresponding to the seven neighbourhoods of Skelmersdale which were grouped round the town centre like spokes on a wheel. The whole town would be served by a team of priests who were committed to the concept of collaborative ministry. At first the team ministry consisted of the priests alone but they were soon joined by some parish sisters active in the different neighbourhoods. Working with key lay-people in each community they shared together in the exercise of collaborative ministry. Seven primary schools were set up and these, for the most part, were the nerve centres of each community where both liturgical and social functions took place. The seven school Heads played a key role in the collaborative ministry. The Skelmersdale Pastoral Council, comprising mainly of two elected representatives from each of the seven communities, had a major role in determining pastoral policy and taking key decisions affecting all seven eucharistic communities.

This account of an experience in collaborative ministry might seem to be dated since it describes a very particular situation at a precise moment in time. Nevertheless, I believe that it still retains its value since it offers an instructive example of collaborative ministry in action. In many ways, the kind of ministry which was being developed in Skelmersdale in the eighties is a prototype of the form of collaborative ministry recommended by the Bishops' Conference of England and Wales in the Report from their Working Party on Collaborative Ministry, *The Sign We Give*.[2] The highly developed form of collaborative ministry which thrived in Skelmersdale in the seventies and eighties has diminished considerably in recent years. Is this a natural progression in collaborative ministry and only to be expected with the passing of time and changing circumstances? Or is it a retrograde step due to administrative decisions about reducing clergy numbers? Or is it linked to appointment procedures or even deliberate changes of policy? Although I do not discuss these questions, it seems to me that if these changes took place without proper consultation, we are only really paying lip-service to collaborative ministry. Maybe I myself have to face that question with regard to my own decision in 1985 to resign from being Team Leader and move from Skelmersdale when I found it impossible to make space for theological and ethical reflection on the enriching experience I was involved in! Though collaborative ministry has far-reaching structural and organisational implications, it is also, and perhaps even more importantly, a state of mind. As I remark towards the end of this chapter, an essential characteristic of this frame of mind is 'respectful and attentive listening in order to empower people to accept fully their own worth and share their gifts for the benefit of all.'

Part 2 moves on to examine certain creative tensions in pastoral ministry. I have preferred to use the expression 'creative tensions' rather than 'problems'. It brings out more forcefully the important truth that we have to live our lives from where we are. Even very difficult situations can contain within them seeds of future hope. Some writers have suggested that not only the Church but even society in general is going through a kind of 'dark night' experience. The chapters in this second part of the book face up to some aspects of the shadow side of pastoral ministry and life in the Church. However, they are written in a spirit of hope and trust in the presence and action of God's Spirit in the Church and in the world.

Chapter 4 is entitled 'Pastoral Ministry and Church Law: 'Mind the Gap'. None of us will deny that at times there can be a clear gap between the faith we profess with our lips and what is going on in our lives. This is brought out vividly by Michael Paul Gallagher in his book, *Questions of Faith*, when he mentions a striking comment made in conversation by the Canadian writer, Northop Frye, 'You don't believe what you say you believe but only what you live.'[3] There can be a gap between the words we use to profess our faith and the way we live our lives. However, the gap can work the other way round, and that is the issue faced in Chapter 4. Then it is not a matter of our lives betraying the faith we profess in word. Instead, it is a matter of our theological formulations lagging behind the richness of our lives and failing to do justice to what our experience leads us to recognise as being from God. People often complain about a gap between so-called 'academic theology' and the truth as experienced by ordinary people on the ground, whether priests, religious or lay. A similar point is made about some of the Church's directives on sacramental ministry and practice, and its rulings on some very practical moral issues. This is a problem which deeply concerns many priests and others working in the field of pastoral ministry. Tragically, what seems to be required by the Church's law often appears to be contrary to what is indicated by a sensitive pastoral reading of a particular situation. In 1995 the National Conference of Priests (NCP) passed a resolution which highlighted 'the growing gap between the official regulations of the church and the demands of pastoral practice.' Much of Chapter 4 was originally written in response to a request from their steering committee for a working paper on this topic which would help the priests wrestle with this urgent and difficult problem. The approach I outline might seem very radical to some. In fact, it is very traditional since it draws on the important notion of *epikeia* which, for Aquinas, was an important dimension of the virtue of justice. This virtue of *epikeia* consists in a person's sensitivity and aptitude in discerning those particular situations in which strict adherence to the law (which, of its very nature, has to be universal) would actually work to the detriment of the value which this specific law has been designed to serve. Bearing in mind the NCP resolution, I describe *epikeia*, understood in this traditional way, as 'the gap virtue'.

The final paragraph of this chapter is drawn from a paper which has a very different origin. I was approached by the secretariat of the Bishops' Conference of England and Wales and asked to write a short reflection as a background paper to help them think about their ministry of promoting communion. I suggested to them that this ministry might best be shown in helping priests and pastoral ministers in their struggle to build communion in pastoral situations where people are feeling alienated and excluded, and where this is at least partly due to an over-rigidity in the application of Church law. This would seem to be far more important than any 'do not rock the boat' approach to communion in the Church. Owing to an administrative confusion, my pastoral reflection paper never actually got into the hands of the bishops. Although Chapter 4 is the shortest chapter in the book, I do not believe that is any indication of its relative importance.

In Chapter 5 I put forward some ideas which I shared first with the Bishops of England and Wales in 1975 when they were kind enough to come to the Upholland Northern Institute for the very first in-service training course run by the newly formed Upholland team. The course was planned collaboratively by a group representing both the bishops and the resident Upholland team and the theme chosen was 'The Bishop as Teacher'. That was also the title of the topic on which I was asked to address the bishops. Anyone familiar with the writings of Karl Rahner will discern the strong influence of his thought in the position I put forward. I apply the concept of collaborative ministry to the teaching ministry in the Church. The teacher is not the fount of all wisdom. In fact, the teacher in the Church is the Holy Spirit. Part of the role of teaching authority is to ensure that the richness of wisdom that the Spirit is sharing is heard by all in the Church. Just as the role of the seminar leader is to make sure that the riches of understanding found in the whole seminar group are made available to all, so an important part of the role of teaching authority in the Church is to make sure that the riches of theological understanding, spiritual insight and ethical discernment found dispersed throughout the Church are made available to the whole Body. This is exactly what happened at the Second Vatican Council. I believe that the greatest exercise of teaching authority in the Church this century was the calling of the Second Vatican Council by Pope John XXIII.

As we saw with reference to Chapter 4, not infrequently there can be a gap between official Church rulings or moral directives and the experience of ordinary people. Why this is so is a complex issue. The notion of 'sensus fidelium' ('the faith instinct of ordinary Christians as a whole') is a difficult theological tool to handle, but nevertheless it remains an important issue. Sometimes the institution needs more time to process experience or our interpretation of experience can be distorted by dehumanising cultural trends. Personal or communal sinfulness is also a factor that can come into the equation. This is even true with regard to the Church as an institution and those with the unenviable responsibility of exercising the Church's teaching ministry. I try to explore this very delicate issue frankly, honestly and charitably in Chapter 6. Writing it made me even more conscious of my own failings and inadequacy.

In his address to the bishops at the opening of the second session of Vatican II, Pope Paul VI said:

> We have just spoken of the Bride of Christ looking upon Christ to discern in him her true likeness. If in doing so she were to discover some shadow, some defect, some stain upon her wedding garment, what should be her instinctive, courageous reaction? There can be no doubt that her primary duty would be to reform, correct and set herself aright in conformity with her divine model.[4]

Chapter 6 examines the delicate issue of the sinfulness of the Church and the need for this to be faced up to with great openness and honesty. This is a matter of pastoral urgency since it affects the very credibility of the Church's teaching and witness. As Karl Rahner has reminded us, there is no disembodied metaphysical Church existing in some ideal order. We, the members of the Church, actually are the Church. Our sins are sins of the Church.

This means that we all, in our different ways, share responsibility both for the effectiveness (or otherwise) of the Church's mission and witness to the world. Responsibility brings with it accountability. If what we do or say renders the Church's mission and witness less credible, the other members of the Church can call us to account for that. Of course, such accountability may be of minor importance in the case of the average Christian whose life might impact on a comparatively small number of people. However, accountability is a matter of much graver importance in the case of those who are responsible for determining the Church's pastoral policies or for formulating and proclaiming the Church's teaching, especially as it affects important issues of personal or social ethics touching the lives of many people. To recognise that those bearing the heavy burden of such a responsibility are sinful like the rest of us is not to imply that they are necessarily personally culpable for the evil consequences of their sin-affected policy decisions and teaching statements. God alone can judge that. Nevertheless, the words of Paul VI to the Vatican II bishops still apply. Sin has to be recognised and owned, especially when it tarnishes the image of the Church. Where those exercising such high responsibility fail to recognise (and so 'own') their sin, it is important that it is named and 'owned' by others in the Church. It is only by recognising and owning it that it becomes possible to 'disown' it and acknowledge it as being in contradiction to what the Church is about. Chapter 6 explores this difficult topic in much greater detail, even facing the possibility that certain Vatican pastoral policy decisions and declarations in the field of ethical teaching may be 'sin-affected'. If this is so, love of the Church would seem to require that such 'sin-affectedness' be both 'owned' and 'disowned' so that the Church's mission and witness may be more credible in today's world. The current teaching on contraception, homosexual relations and second marriage after divorce are seen as possible examples of such 'sin-affected' teaching.

In one way or another the five chapters which make up Part

3 discuss issues related to the way moral theology can provide a service to help those working in the field of pastoral ministry.

Chapter 7 looks at how moral theology can be helpful in pastoral ministry in the parish setting. Prior to Vatican II the role of moral theology in the parish was principally to do with equipping priests to be competent confessors by training them to distinguish the different kinds of sins people were likely to confess and to make a judgement on their gravity. It also helped priests to be compassionate confessors by showing them how to recognise and make allowances for the many extenuating factors present in people's lives which might diminish their culpability for sins confessed. All this involved listening to people. However, from the very nature of the case this listening tended to be focused on people's sins. In this chapter I suggest that moral theology has an even more important role in helping people appreciate the giftedness and goodness in their lives, even when this may be hidden to some extent by the legacy of 'strangling weeds' they may have inherited from wounding experiences in early life or even from failures and sins long repented.

This chapter also challenges the assumption that moral theology is all about principles and rules, whereas pastoral theology enables us to cope with the exceptions and helps us to be compassionate in our ministry. I argue that of its very nature moral theology is pastoral. It not only allows for exceptions; its very development as a science is largely dependent on our learning from the 'good conscience' exceptions we experience in the course of our everyday lives. A moral theology which is pastorally sensitive and open to learning from experience is also fully at home with the phenomenon of moral and spiritual growth in the midst of all the ambiguities of a person's life. In writing this chapter I was deeply moved by the parable of the wheat growing among the darnel. The owner of the field is concerned lest the miracle of the wheat's growth be threatened with destruction by the misguided zeal of the workers wanting to drag out the darnel, regardless of the harm they might cause to the wheat. My pastoral experience has made me more and more convinced of what I write towards the end of this chapter: 'Sometimes what might look like a puny and undeveloped plant might, in fact, be a miracle of growth, given the adverse conditions under which it has had to struggle.'[5]

The world in which pastoral ministry takes place has changed dramatically over recent years. As a result, the very nature of pastoral ministry itself has undergone a radical reappraisal. As we have seen with reference to earlier chapters, pastoral ministry today must necessarily take the form of collaborative ministry and this concept has implications even for the pastoral ministry of offering authoritative teaching in the Church. In this changing situation it is only to be expected that moral theology will also be the subject of important changes which, in turn, will have an impact on the exercise of pastoral ministry in the parish.

In Chapter 8 I don my specialist hat as a moral theologian and offer a personal view of how I have experienced the changes which have taken place in moral theology during my forty years as a priest whose ministry has always involved working as a moral theologian in some way or other. I look at nine influential factors which, to my mind, have had a major impact on moral theology in recent years.

The person-centred moral theology of Vatican II leads the list with its insistence on the universally applicable ethical criterion of the dignity of the human person, integrally and adequately considered. Second on my list comes the essential contribution to moral theology issuing from the experience and reflection of women. This is urgently needed to restore the balance after centuries of male-dominated moral theology. I believe that the implications of this change will be far-reaching and some of them probably impossible for most of us to imagine. The ecumenical dimension comes third on my list, presenting a particular challenge to the Roman Catholic Church with its traditional style of clear-cut, definitive moral teaching. This also links in with some of the points covered in Chapter 6 regarding the implications of our acknowledging that we are a sinful Church when it comes to the exercise of the Church's teaching ministry.

The fourth factor generating far-reaching changes in the field of moral theology is the explosion of our empirical knowledge and the consequent advances in human technology. Today we are having to face complex ethical issues which moral theologians of an earlier age would never have dreamt of. Fifth on my list comes a cultural factor of major importance: the development of historical consciousness. That is not just a matter of our knowing more about past history. Rather, it is a growing appreciation of the fact that who we are as persons and the world we now live in are largely the product of history. Consequently, in the very process of living, we are actually fashioning history in the making and even now are making our mark on what will happen in the future. This historical consciousness makes us aware that many of what we have regarded as basic institutions of life are subject to historical and cultural influences and thus open to critical reassessment. Vatican II's criterion of the dignity of the human person, integrally and adequately considered, is a constant challenge to human cultures and historical forms, even though our very understanding of this criterion is necessarily culturally and historically conditioned. This leads into the sixth factor which is changing the face of moral theology, namely the place of human experience in moral theology. This is brought out clearly, with particular reference to medical ethics, in the already-quoted comment of Jack Mahoney. To ignore human experience will inevitably result in that pastorally harmful 'gap' which was examined earlier.

My final three factors which have occasioned changes in moral theology are all to do with the way the role of moral theologians has been affected by issues related to communication. In the first place, moral theologians today must engage in dialogue with a whole variety of different groups. As we have seen already, other Christian Churches must be dialogue partners. Likewise, other faiths need to be involved, and the dialogue must be interdisciplinary too. Failure to respect this mode will disqualify a moral theologian from the right to be listened to by other partners in dialogue.

Many of the new issues on the moral theology agenda today are matters of public concern and are often aired in the media. Moral theologians would seem to be evading their responsibility if they refuse to get involved in public debate on such burning issues. However, one of the key rules of public debate is that participants must be open and honest. This means that a moral theologian must not bracket out his or her critical judgement when interviewed by the media. Where a Church statement is open to criticism, this must be acknowledged. Otherwise, the search for truth is made to play second fiddle to public relations. Too great a concern not to rock the boat is hardly a convincing witness to the vessel's sea-worthiness!

Finally, I discuss the problems faced by a moral theologian due to the happy situation that we have a Pope who is himself both a philosopher and a moral theologian. John Paul II's encyclical letters dealing with moral issues have been weighty documents. However, the fact that they are written or at least inspired by the Pope does not invest each page with full papal authority. To a certain extent, when the Pope speaks or writes on moral issues, he is doing moral theology in public. Moral theologians show proper respect for his utterances and statements by engaging seriously at a professional level with the views he has expressed and the arguments he has put forward to support them. Failure to do this out of reverence for his position as Pope could lead to what Richard McCormick describes as a 'weakening of the papal magisterium'. An attitude of reverential silence in place of critical engagement would be tantamount to professional irresponsibility on the part of a moral theologian. The same is true with regard to moral theologians and the Congregation for the Doctrine of the Faith (CDF) as I point out in the Epilogue of my *New Directions in Moral Theology: The Challenge of Being Human* which is a constructively critical conversation with 1990 CDF Instruction, 'The Ecclesial Vocation of the Theologian' with special reference to moral theology.

Chapter 9 looks at the Catechism of the Catholic Church as a tool to be used by those engaged in pastoral ministry. It recognises that it was not originally designed for this purpose but was intended for bishops and those working in the field of catechetics to help them compose their own catechisms which would be more suited to their local situation. However, the Catechism's publication in an attractive format has made it available to a much wider public.[6] In fact, in the field of religious publishing it has become a bestseller. Hence, it is important that it should be read in a way which people will find spiritually enriching and pastorally helpful.

In Chapter 9 I focus on the Catechism purely as it touches on the field of morality. It is very significant that Part III of the Catechism, which deals with Christian morality, has the title 'Life in Christ'. When the bishops of the world were consulted about the Catechism, they all emphasised that its treatment of morality should be both positive and inspirational. Their wish is certainly reflected in the title 'Life in Christ' and also in the title of the first of the two sections which make up Part III, namely, 'Our Human Vocation: Life in the Spirit'. In the tips I offer prospective readers for reading the Catechism on morality, I remind them that they need to read all the small print in the light of these positive headings. Even the Ten Commandments (the title of the second section of Part III) should be interpreted in that light. In other words, they should be understood as a charter for positive living and as a reminder to us of the boundaries beyond which life can become inhuman and unloving. I even suggest that readers might find it helpful to try to devise a positive formulation for each of the Ten Commandments and in an appendix to Chapter 9 I offer my own attempt at this exercise. Another basic rule for reading Part III of the Catechism, which the Pope and the bishops have made abundantly clear, is that it should be interpreted in the light of Vatican II and not vice versa. The fact that its publication is later in time than Vatican II does not mean that it can supersede the spirit and teaching of that Council in any way. Consequently among the various tips I offer to prospective readers of the Catechism on morality is a reminder that any interpretation of Christian morality needs to respect Vatican II's commitment to ecumenism. As I note in tip no. 6, 'This implies that, when there are particular issues of moral disagreement between the major Christian Churches, the Catechism's presentation of the current authoritative Catholic teaching should not be presumed to be the final and definitive Christian position on this topic.' In tip no. 9 I remind readers of two fundamental truths in Catholic morality that need to be kept together in creative conflict: the primacy of conscience and the authority of the Church to teach in the field of morality. Tip no. 11 gives a timely reminder that 'the experience and reflection of women have not been adequately represented in the field of moral theology and in the process of formulating moral teaching in the Catholic Church'.

Chapter 10 focuses on the issue of conscience and conscience formation. It challenges immature understandings of conscience which fail to take either life or sin seriously. By ignoring the person-injuring dimension of human evil they take the sting out of sin and allow people to feel complacent as long as they can plead 'not guilty' to the evil they have perpetrated. Conscience formation is presented as becoming increasingly sensitive to the call of God as it comes to us through the humanly inflicted evils we encounter in everyday life. We 'create' God's will by responding to this call to the best of our ability. Conscience, therefore, is not trying to discover some predetermined plan God has laid down for each of us, as though we were merely puppets being manipulated by some kind of divine puppet master. We develop our sensitivity of conscience by becoming more aware of life around us, by seeing the opportunities for making our little corner of God's world a better place in terms of love, justice and peace, and also by opening our ears to the pain of our world.

Taking my cue from the words of Jesus, 'I have come to call not the just but sinners', in Chapter 11 I suggest that the spiritual life is not some esoteric affair reserved for a few unworldly types. Rather it can legitimately be viewed as a lifelong process of growth out of sin which applies to every human person. Because our interdependence affects us from our earliest years, we all emerge from our formative years as both 'victims of sin' and 'inheritors of grace'. Depending on the kind of negative influences we have been touched by and the woundedness of the people who have affected our lives in our developing years, the adults we grow into are a complex mix of light and shade. Our woundedness will be as unique as our gracefulness, since there is something absolutely unique about each of our personal stories. Each of us emerges from childhood with our own unique web of relationships and our own particular set of formative events. Consequently, each of us will have our own specific agenda for our life-long process of growth out of the consequences of our being victims of sin. At the same time, there will be many common features on our different agendas for growth since a considerable part of our woundedness as victims of sin will be due to social factors which many or all of us share in common, for instance, poverty, patriarchy, racism, homophobia, educational disadvantage, etc., etc. Clearly, in the case of such causes of our woundedness, a spirituality of growth out of sin will necessarily include our becoming involved in social and political action in one form or another.

The wounding effect of being victims of sin can disfigure our personal development and so have an influence on our becoming ourselves agents of sin. That, in turn, provides another agenda for our growth out of sin, an agenda which will, to some extent, overlap with our first agenda. This agenda, too, will have its social dimension. Monika Hellwig has remarked that Christians are experiencing a 'shift to an awareness of collective responsibility for individual sins, and individual responsibility for the collective sin.' In the second half of Chapter 11 I try to face the objection that growth out of sin might seem a rather negative starting point for a Christian spirituality. I suggest that a growth out of sin spirituality ties in better with our contemporary understanding of evolution and the whole process of human development, both individual and collective. Of course, I am not suggesting that human history is simply one long uninterrupted story of our natural and steady progress towards becoming more fully human. Far from it! Human history is much more ambiguous. Every apparent advance seems to bring with it new possibilities for our behaving more inhumanly towards ourselves and each other. That is also true with regard to the earth, our common home, and the many other creatures who share this home with us, not to mention the vast spaces beyond our planet. Human progress is far from being a natural and inevitable process in the course of time.

In the final part of Chapter 11 I explore the insight which Albert Nolan draws from his experience in South Africa during the apartheid years: 'sin becomes visible in suffering'.[7] In listening to the cries of human suffering in our world today, we can hear the voice of God calling us to tackle the human causes of much of this suffering. Out of the midst of so much that contradicts and diminishes human life, freedom and love, the creative command of God is heard: 'Let there be life; let there be freedom; let there be love.' That creative command is addressed to us humans, summoning us to continue God's ongoing work of creation. I suggest that a spirituality of growth out of sin is a life-giving spirituality. It is also true to our invitation from Christ to continue his work of healing and liberation. And it is a spirituality fully in line with the command of Jesus that we must love one another as he has loved us.

Part 4 of the book turns its attention to some pastoral and moral questions related to life and death issues. Chapter 12 is a slightly revised version of the text of a talk I gave at Westminster on 6 December 1989 prior to the debate on embryo research. I had been invited by the Institute of Medical Ethics to be one of a panel to 'brief' members on the relevant scientific and ethical aspects of the debate. The other two members of the panel were Professor Mary Sellers and Professor Robert Edwards. The session was open to any Members of both Houses of Parliament who wished to attend. In fact, only six MPs attended the meeting. My brief was to help them appreciate the thinking behind the different ethical views on embryo research found among different Christians and Christian Churches.

After pointing out how expressions like 'You are playing God', or 'slippery slope' arguments, or a too-glib appeal to moral absolutes can cloud rather than clarify a moral issue, I try to establish some common ground based on our shared belief in the dignity of the human person. This means that morality is, therefore, something we recognise and respect, and not something we simply create for ourselves. The main part of the chapter looks at the different ways Christian theologians have tried to ground their conflicting answers to the question 'When did I begin?' Since they are all dealing with the same embryological data and they all subscribe to the God-given dignity of the human person, it is clear that their divergence of view is due to different philosophical positions regarding the degree of embryological development which is essential before a biological 'human life' can truly be said to be an individual person of infinite dignity.

Chapter 13 grew out of the terrible disaster which had such a profound impact on the city of Liverpool when, on 15 April 1989, many young Liverpool supporters died tragically at Hillsborough football stadium. For the family of Tony Bland the Hillsborough disaster followed a different course. Although he did not die in the crush, he was so badly injured that after some time he was diagnosed as being in the persistent vegetative state (PVS). His parents eventually came to the conclusion that the most appropriate loving care for Tony was to cease the medical procedure of artificial nutrition and hydration which was the only way he could be kept alive, and let him die naturally. However, they and the doctor caring for Tony were warned that the law was unclear on this point and they might be laying themselves open to a charge of murder. In the end the decision given by the Law Lords on Tony's case allowed the withdrawal of artificial nutrition and hydration, thereby arousing further controversy. To believe, as I do, that their decision was right, is not to accept all the arguments they adduced in its favour.

In the meantime, the issue had also been hotly debated in the public forum. In the United States, where some fairly similar cases had hit the headlines, a few Roman Catholic theologians maintained that the withdrawal of artificial nutrition and hydration was tantamount to starving a person to death and should be rejected as ethically unacceptable. Richard McCormick, a Jesuit and the leading U.S. exponent of Roman Catholic medical ethics, strongly rejected their position. He argued that such withdrawal in properly diagnosed cases of PVS was fully in keeping with the traditional principles of Catholic medical ethics. He suggested that those opposed to withdrawal have 'slipped their grasp on the heart of the Catholic tradition in this matter.'[8] In the UK, some of those who opposed the withdrawal of artificial nutrition and hydration from Tony Bland, seemed to be making the same mistake. This chapter combines parts of two articles I was prompted to write on the Tony Bland case: 'A Medical Dilemma' and 'Rest for Tony Bland'.[9]

In the course of this chapter I examine the rich tradition in Roman Catholic moral and pastoral theology which relates to the appropriate care for the dying. Once again, it is a tradition based on the dignity of the human person. How can a person be best helped to live this final stage of his or her life with dignity – and eventually die with dignity? To make one's main priority that of preserving life for as long as possible is to opt for a moral criterion which fails to embrace the good of the human person, integrally and adequately considered. It is to turn a person's bodily existence into an idol. The genuine Roman Catholic tradition in medical ethics recognises the historical dimension of our being human persons and so respects all the stages of human life, including the final stage of dying. Such a holistic approach does not attempt to prolong the dying process for as long as possible. It means helping a person pass through the dying process in a way which respects his or her dignity as a person. This has implications for pain relief, even when this may have the indirect effect of shortening life. It also implies that we do not try to resuscitate when this offers no appreciative benefit to the person or is clearly contrary to his or her wishes. In reality, both the hospice movement and the growing emphasis on palliative care and its spiritual dimension are based on a similar commitment to the dignity of the human person during the closing stages of life. Although this chapter was prompted by a concern lest the response to the Tony Bland case failed to do justice to the full riches of our medical ethics tradition, the issues covered go far beyond Tony Bland. They are also based on what I have learnt from people during my years in a parish where a good part of my time involved the pastoral ministry of being with families during the precious time when they were caring for a family member who was dying.

The final chapter deals with the HIV/AIDS pandemic, particularly the devastating impact it is having on many developing countries. This might seem a strange topic with which to conclude a book entitled *From a Parish Base* and dealing mainly with issues of moral and pastoral theology as they affect pastoral ministry in a parish context. However, one of the main points I am making in this chapter is that tackling some of the main causes responsible for the rapid spread of HIV/AIDS in the developing world demands a radical conversion of thinking and lifestyle on the part of those of us who live in the so-called developed world. Perhaps this chapter is an ideal conclusion to a book which begins 'from a parish base'. It reminds us that pastoral theology cannot be 'parochial' in the narrow sense of that word. Our interdependence has global implications. If it is true to say, as I suggest, that both our human family and the body of Christ has AIDS, then in a very real sense we are all of us 'living with AIDS'. Whether we live positively or negatively with AIDS is the pastoral challenge.

Most of the chapters in this book have their origin in articles which I initially wrote for *The Tablet, The Month, The Way, The Way Supplement* and *Priests and People.*[10] I am most grateful to their editors, John Wilkins, Tim Noble, Jackie Hawkins and David Sanders, for permission to use the material drawn from the various articles in question. I am also grateful for the help and encouragement the editors of these periodicals gave me when they first suggested that I should write on these important topics in the field of moral and pastoral theology. In a very real sense they have played an important part in the long process leading up to the publication of this book. I would also like to thank the editor of *New Blackfriars* for permission to use part of an article which originally appeared in that journal. At the beginning of each chapter, I have acknowledged in which of these periodicals these essays first appeared in their original form. For inclusion in this volume some of the original articles have undergone considerable editorial change, others have needed only very minor editorial adjustment.

Finally, I am grateful to Morag Reeve, Editorial Director of Darton, Longman and Todd. When I was looking for a home for this book, she welcomed me with open arms and has been very patient and helpful in the process of preparing the manuscript for publication against the pressure of a fairly tight schedule.

PART 1

Parish-based Pastoral Ministry

1

From Vatican II into the Millennium: Blueprint for a Contemporary Parish

Archbishop Worlock based his whole ministry in Liverpool on the vision of the mission of the Church found in Vatican II. That inspired all he did as Archbishop. In this he led from the front. I hope it is no disrespect to Derek's memory to recognise that his leadership from the front was both a strength and a weakness. It was a strength when he was trying to offer a practical example of what life in the post-Vatican II church should really be like. Hence, his collaborative ministry with David Sheppard and the other Church leaders on Merseyside was a lived out challenge to all of us to look at our own ecumenical relationships. His leadership from the front was also a strength when it enabled a rapid human and Christian response to be made in the face of terrible tragedies such as Hillsborough or social issues calling for speedy intervention on the part of the Churches. Another way in which his leadership from the front was a strength was when it was directed towards empowering priests and lay-people in the Church to be able to collaborate in the Church's ministry. In these and other ways leadership from the front can be necessary when a major change of direction is called for.

On the weakness side, in today's vision of Church, there is a certain incongruity about a bishop leading too strongly from the front! In the case of Derek, at times his leadership from the front could be somewhat overpowering and almost too efficient. Like

---

This is an abbreviated version of an essay which first appeared in *The Month*, April 1996, 129-36, under the title 'Archbishop Worlock's Legacy to Liverpool'.

many leaders, Archbishop Worlock must have been torn between his commitment to collaborative ministry (people power) and his natural inclination towards the most efficient way to achieve results. Results are important but so is the empowerment of people. Derek Worlock's dilemma lay in the fact that he firmly believed in the empowerment of people but he also believed that he had the power, in his personal capacity as Archbishop, to influence major socio-political decisions to improve housing, employment, education, health and environment prospects for people in Liverpool. And all these levels of improvement could help to empower people by raising their standard of living. In the case of the Eldonians in the Vauxhall district of Liverpool (cf. Chapter 2), he managed to get the balance just right. He supported them fully in their exercise of 'people power' while using his influence in the corridors of power at certain key moments when this was both appropriate and necessary.

This chapter will focus on six dimensions of the church's life and mission which, I believe, summed up Derek Worlock's vision of the church for today. They are the following:

1. a church committed to furthering the coming of the Kingdom in society;
2. a sacramental church;
3. an inclusive church;
4. an ecumenical church;
5. a catholic church;
6. a praying and worshipping church.

Building on but moving beyond the post-Vatican II vision of the church this list offers one picture of what a parish might look like as we approach the millennium. It is not the only possible scenario. Others might see things differently. The rest of this chapter will amplify each of these six dimensions and offer some concrete suggestions as to how they might affect parish life.

A church committed to furthering the coming of the Kingdom in society

Derek Worlock took to heart the words of the 1971 Synod,

Justice in the World: 'Action on behalf of justice and participation in the transformation of the world fully appear to us as a constitutive dimension of the preaching of the Gospel, or, in other words, of the Church's mission for the redemption of the human race and its liberation from every oppressive situation.'[1] He understood that to mean that the church is not a mutual assurance club to serve the interests of its members. Its very *raison d'être* lies in its mission to society and to the world. The key Vatican II Constitution, *Lumen Gentium*, expressed this in slightly different language when it opened its reflection on the church by defining it as 'a kind of sacrament or sign of intimate union with God, and of the unity of all human kind' and as 'an instrument for the achievement of such union and unity' (n.1). Vatican II's vision is not one of a 'churchy' church but of a 'worldly' church. The church exists to serve the world. An essential part of its service lies in 'action on behalf of justice' and 'liberation from every oppressive situation'.

Issues of social justice were a major concern to Derek in his ministry as Archbishop of Liverpool. From his earliest days as a priest he had always been a great believer in the Young Christian Workers (YCW) and made many life-long friends among workers in that movement. He continued that support and friendship as they moved into the adult Family and Social Apostolate (FSA) and its successor, the Movement of Christian Workers (MCW). So it came naturally to him, along with Bishop Sheppard, to campaign forcefully against political and industrial decisions that had disastrous effects on the lives of working men and women – and those without work too. He also recognised that people's right to proper housing and adequate health care was an urgent matter of social justice in a city like Liverpool. So, too, was rooting out the causes of racial injustice and creating a more equal society.

Part of Derek's legacy is to challenge us with the question: do we want a church which understands preaching the gospel as involving 'action on behalf of justice and participation in the transformation of the world' and which sees its mission as embracing 'liberation from every oppressive situation'? Lest we say 'yes' too glibly, it is worth reminding ourselves what this is likely to mean in practice.

I suggest that the following are just a few of the things it could mean in terms of parish life:

- a parish organised according to the understanding that it is principally in the local neighbourhood and not in the church and church societies that the work of building God's Kingdom is, or is not, taking place;
- a parish which judges its fidelity to living the gospel by the extent that its members are willing to play an active part in the local community rather than by whether they are regular attenders at mass;
- a parish where the victims of oppression can feel at home and where the perpetrators of oppression feel disturbed and challenged;
- a parish in which the homily is not reduced to an other-worldly spiritual message but where it resonates with the nitty-gritty of people's everyday lives, raising up the down-hearted and overturning the mighty;
- a parish which is automatically involved in the social analysis of the causes of local injustices or other issues of community concern, whether in the field of housing, (un)employment, health care, welfare provision, education, drug addiction, nursery provision etc.;
- a parish where women feel they belong, not because they are presumed to be naturally pious, but because they sense that their oppression and exploitation as women is recognised and is treated as a matter of serious concern;
- a parish where gays and lesbians can feel secure, because their dignity as human persons is fully accepted, their struggle to live out loving and faithful relationships is appreciated and celebrated, and the pain and injustice they have suffered through homophobia is acknowledged, even to the extent of guilt being confessed and forgiveness requested;
- a parish where the sale of Catholic papers is of much less concern than the manipulation of the media by powerful vested interests and the consequent distortion of vision unjustly foisted upon readers and viewers.

Although I am not suggesting that Archbishop Worlock would

have given his personal support to all of the above, I believe they are all in line with the fundamental vision of the church put forward by Vatican II, a vision which was his inspiration as Archbishop of Liverpool.

A sacramental church

By 'sacramental' church I do not simply mean a church in which the sacraments are administered and which is a model in fulfilling all the latest liturgical directives. I mean a church which recognises that the whole of life is sacramental. This is, in other words, a church which believes that the presence and action of God are mediated to us through the daily humdrum of our everyday lives. A sacramental church helps people to become aware of the presence of God 'deep down things', as Gerard Manley Hopkins so succinctly expressed it. Derek Worlock believed in that kind of church. His concern for the liturgy was not simply at the level of external form and beauty, important though he believed those to be. He wanted the liturgy to be in touch with what was going on in the depths of people's hearts. The external form and beauty provided the atmosphere conducive to let that happen, rather than the reality itself.

Vatican II's choice metaphor for the church was 'the people of God'. While that metaphor brings out very forcefully the truth that we are all the church and that ministry is for service, not selective streaming, in the church, it also evokes the immanence of God in the depths of all people. Hence, it is intimately bound up with the sacramentality of the church in the way I have described it above. This sacramentality is even more fundamental to the church than its hierarchical character.

What would a parish be like which was sacramental in this sense? Again, I offer a few suggestions drawn from among many possibilities:

- a parish in which the priest is not a cleric, confined within a functional role imposed on him by the institution (and perhaps by some strong-minded parishioners!), but instead can feel free to help people discern what is going on deep in their lives and to follow where the Spirit is moving them, even if this does not easily fit into the usual institutional categories;

- a parish in which creativity and imagination (neither of which is synonymous with gimmickry) are used in a spirit of responsible freedom in the preparation and celebration of the liturgy so that it resonates with whatever is affecting people most profoundly in their lives or is of deep concern to the community as a whole;
- a parish with a genuine respect for the consciences of individuals, recognising the uniqueness of each person and his or her life, and aware that each person's journey through life follows its own special route with all the ups and downs of the dying-and-rising process peculiar to the story of this unique individual;
- a parish which believes so strongly in the Holy Spirit that it has the courage to trust the movement of God's Spirit in the lives of its members; and which also believes that this one Spirit we all share may, at times, lead us to challenge and be challenged by each other.

Once again, I would not want to claim Derek Worlock's explicit approval for each of the above suggestions. However, I remember very vividly his homily to the Liverpool delegates to the Pastoral Congress a few weeks before it took place. He told us that some people had said to him: 'Are you not afraid of gathering three thousand people together to talk about the Church and its mission? You don't know what might happen.' His reply to them was: 'Don't you trust the Holy Spirit?' That was his vision of the post-Vatican II church.

An inclusive church

Here again the Vatican II metaphor of the People of God contains the germ for the inclusive image of the church. Inclusive here is a very rich concept. It implies the inclusion of people's giftedness in the ministry of the church. This lies at the heart of collaborative ministry, something to which Derek was totally committed though not always able to implement. A striking example of his commitment to collaborative ministry is the fact that the Working Party Report on Collaborative Ministry, *The Sign We Give*, issued last year by the Bishops' Conference, was largely the work of Pat Jones, a young Liverpool lay-woman. Due to Derek's influence and strong support, collaborative ministry for Pat for many years meant that she was deeply involved in the episcopal ministry of the Bishops' Conference through her role as its Assistant General Secretary.

An inclusive church is also a church where everyone can feel at home and no one feels excluded. Evidence of Derek's commitment to such a church was seen at the October 1994 session of the Liverpool Archdiocesan Pastoral Council where delegates were invited to a 'listening session' entitled 'How I feel about the Church'. It enabled people who often feel marginalised in the church to share their feelings and experience with delegates and tell them what needed to happen if they were to feel really included in the church. Among the speakers were a gay man, a divorced woman, two people representing marginalised young people and a priest who felt most of his ministry was on the margins of the church.

The following are a few indications of what a parish might be like if it tried to live out this vision of an inclusive church:

- a parish totally committed to collaborative ministry. Therefore, a parish in which the parish priest sees himself and is seen by parishioners as a team leader and in which the team he leads is not a chosen few but represents all who are exercising any kind of ministry in the parish. In fact, the team members should themselves be team leaders in an ever-increasing series of concentric circles of shared ministry. Moreover, ministry here is interpreted in a very wide sense, including, for instance, parents, teachers, people caring for sick or aging relatives at home, etc.;
- a parish in which decision-making is not exclusively in the hands of the parish priest but is shared and spread through the concentric circles of collaborative ministry, due account being taken of the principle of subsidiarity, the need for competence, co-operation, consistency, accountability and, when appropriate, specialised knowledge;
- a parish which has been able to work out its own mission

statement which has been owned by all its members, so that there is a common vision and sense of purpose in the ministry in which people are collaborating and so that the life and mission of the parish is not dependent on the whims or prejudices of any incoming priest;

- a parish in which those who often feel marginalised in church and society are able to feel at home and have a sense of belonging; hence, a parish in which there is a welcoming forum where those who feel excluded are given a sympathetic hearing; which, in turn, means a parish which is not afraid of criticism, even self-criticism, and which is prepared to change anything in its lifestyle which tends to exclude rather than include people;
- a parish which has a problem with being asked to pray for vocations by a Church which, through its exclusion of women from the priesthood, refuses to believe that God might be calling them to this form of ministry.

An ecumenical church

No one can deny that the post-Vatican II church is called to be an ecumenical church. Derek Worlock certainly embraced this vision of an ecumenical church. The close friendship between the Archbishop and Bishop Sheppard (and his wife, Grace) was a very public sign of his commitment to such a church. Moreover, rather than seeing themselves as a double act, they made sure it was all the Church leaders on Merseyside who were involved.

Though he was prepared to leave the precise form Christian unity might take in the hands of the Lord, there is no doubt that this was something Derek dearly *longed for* with all his heart. Hence, we need to use our imagination again in an effort to see what sort of parish we should *want* if we are to be true to this dimension of the post-Vatican II vision of the church. Once again, a few very personal suggestions might stimulate us to think further about this:

- a parish in which the parish leaders have developed a good working relationship, a sense of mutual trust and friendship and a shared concern for the church's mission in the neighbourhood with the leaders of the other local Christian churches through meeting regularly to share in prayer, collaborative planning and to develop personal and denominational understanding and friendship;

- a parish which is fully committed to the principle that nothing should be done separately which can be done at least equally well together;
- a parish where ecumenical co-operation and friendship is not the sole preserve of the parish leaders but where all parishioners are enabled to have the opportunity to meet their non-Catholic Christian sisters and brothers through shared worship in each other's churches, through actively collaborating with each other in ministry and mission and through developing closer understanding and friendship by means of ecumenical house groups or joint social gatherings;
- a parish which is prepared to tackle the structural obstacles to ecumenical progress; making sure, for instance, that church schools foster ecumenical understanding and association rather than consolidate disunity by keeping children separate; that inter-church marriages are welcomed as exciting experiments in Christian unity already achieved;
- a parish which refuses to accept any implication that intercommunion is shocking and scandalous but which believes that it is actually called for by the very meaning of the Eucharist; hence, a parish which is unhappy with the norms on eucharistic sharing issued by the Catholic Bishops' Conferences of England and Wales, Ireland and Scotland in their 1998 teaching document *One Bread One Body*, believing that the main thrust of eucharistic theology is not towards defining boundaries of exclusion but towards stretching inclusion to the furthest limits which are consonant with safeguarding the essentials of unity; a parish, therefore, which is anxious that the possibilities of eucharistic intercommunion envisaged in n. 129 of the 1993 Ecumenical Directory be extended as widely as possible.

A catholic church

Catholic, as we have all been taught, means universal. Vatican II stressed the catholicity of the church in a whole variety of ways. For instance, its teaching on collegiality among the bishops emphasised that the pastoral responsibility of bishops was not confined within the boundaries of their own dioceses. Derek Worlock lived this out not only at national level through the major role he played in the Bishops' Conference over many years, but also at an international level. Moreover, he encouraged Liverpool priests and lay-people to be truly catholic in their faith by enabling them to work in Latin America through the establishment of the Latin American Missionary Project (LAMP), a project which was dear to his heart and which took its toll on his health.

What are the implications for parish life of Derek's post-Vatican II vision of a church which is truly catholic? Again, I offer a few suggestions as to what a parish would be like which is trying to be true to that vision:

- a parish which is not too 'parochial' in its concerns; and hence:
- a parish which is prepared to accept that parish interests need not be the only or even the determining factor in some difficult decisions affecting it – for instance, amalgamating or even closing a parish school; losing one of its priests or even sharing its only priest with another parish; giving up its presbytery or even its church; sharing the financial burdens of less well-off parishes; or even the extreme case of ceasing to exist as a parish in order to merge with another parish or to embark on a more experimental form of local church community;
- a parish in which justice and peace issues, at home or abroad, are the concern of the whole parish and not just of the select few in the local J & P group, and this being reflected in the liturgy, educational programmes and financial priorities of the parish;
- a parish which is well-informed about what is happening, positively and negatively, in the wider Church; and hence:

- a parish which instinctively networks with positive Church initiatives nationally and internationally;
- and a parish in which concern is felt and expressed about injustice within the church, as well as in society, and in which respect for the Pope and his ministry of communion among the Churches is not understood as meaning an uncritical response to everything emanating from the Vatican.

A praying and worshipping church

A close friend of Derek's told me recently that the reason why she invited him to be godfather of one of her daughters was because he was 'a good pray-er'. Though Derek, like all of us, may have had his shortcomings, lack of commitment to prayer was not one of them. Those who were close to him bear ample witness to that. True to the vision of the Vatican II church, he was also a firm believer in liturgical prayer. Derek also had the rare gift of being able to sense when the feelings of a whole community needed to be expressed through the deeply-felt solidarity of some kind of shared act of prayer. The prime example of that was the hastily arranged but very inspirational mass at the Liverpool Metropolitan Cathedral on the evening after the Hillsborough disaster. This gave the whole city of Liverpool the opportunity to share its sense of shock and draw comfort from this powerfully symbolic assurance that God was there with them in the darkness of their grief and suffering.

Obviously, prayer and worship are essential parts of the life of every parish. Still, it is worth using our pastoral imagination to envisage additional ways in which a parish can be true to Vatican II's call to be a praying and worshipping community:

- a parish which puts more emphasis on prayer, than on prayers;
- a parish in which spending time in prayer is a natural expectation for anyone prepared to involve themselves in the more organised collaborative ministry in the parish;
- a parish in which the priest, in particular, is a good pray-er, giving prayer a high priority in his daily horarium, feeding his prayer and preaching through scriptural and other

nourishing reading and allowing himself sufficient space for solitude and retreat;

- a parish where the deep human events in the lives of individuals, families and the community are allowed sensitive and meaningful expression in the liturgy; and hence:
- a parish where it is recognised that the priest needs at least as much preparation for the celebration of a baptism, marriage or funeral as do the people themselves, a preparation which enables him to tune into the deeper human meaning of this event in their lives; hence:
- a parish where families experience the funeral liturgy as an authentic and very personal celebration of the life of whoever has died, as well as a faith-filled support and comfort for them in their grief;
- a parish where the language used in the baptism of a child, as well as expressing its deep theological significance, also enables the parents and family to celebrate the birth of their child, to thank God for entrusting this precious gift to their care and to commit themselves as parents and family to his or her upbringing as a Christian human person;
- a parish where the preparation for and celebration of a marriage clearly recognise that this is a key moment in the growth of a couple's love for each other, enabling them to pledge and celebrate that love publicly and affirming them in their faith and courage to continue on their exciting but difficult journey together; hence:
- a preparation and celebration which feel no need to express any condemnation of the couple if they have been cohabiting up to this point but which is able to rejoice with them in the goodness they have experienced in their shared love and which is also able to feel at ease with the active participation in the wedding of any children who may already be the fruit of that love;
- a parish in which the full and active participation of the people, as demanded by Vatican II, is the top priority in liturgical celebration and in which more detailed liturgical regulations are kept subservient to this top priority; hence:
- a parish which feels not only free but even obliged to bend

the letter of the liturgical law in order to achieve its authentic spirit, even when this involves such practices as general absolution and the careful adaptation or even composition of eucharistic prayers for particular occasions.

As in the previous sections, I would not claim Derek's imprimatur for all the above suggestions. I believe, however, that they fit in with the vision of post-Vatican II church to which he was so totally committed.

Conclusion: Meeting the unpredictable future 'with hope in our hearts'

It would be presumptuous to be too specific about the kind of church God is calling us to be. Throughout this chapter I have consistently taken for granted the ongoing existence of the parish. Though it is hard to envisage any Christian alternative to the gathered community of people in a locality, whether we call it parish or not, God's Spirit could possibly be demanding a depth of dying and rising in the Church which is beyond our present understanding. Even in the face of such a prospect, Derek Worlock, with his friend, David Sheppard, would urge us to go forward 'with hope in our hearts', to quote the title of the final book they wrote together in 1994.[2]

2

Struggling to Live the Gospel in Inner-city Liverpool: a Case Study

The Eldonian community in Liverpool

The Eldonians are not a religious community. They are a group of ordinary people, families, single men and women, young and old, who live in the Vauxhall area of inner-city Liverpool. Where they live takes in some of the north docklands and it includes but is not co-extensive with the parish of Our Lady's, Eldon Street.

Although they would not describe themselves as a Catholic body, virtually all the Eldonians are Catholics since their ancestors were mostly Irish and Italian, and a few Polish, immigrants who settled in this part of Liverpool at the time of the Irish famine.[1] The area soon became very densely populated. The housing conditions, health provision and sanitation were appalling and there was great poverty among the people. Living conditions improved somewhat over the years but life continued to be hard. Very large families were still living in inadequately-sized flats in tenement blocks. Most of the men worked on the docks or in dock-related industries; many of the women had to combine looking after the home and the children with working in the factories or in cleaning jobs of one kind or another. The area suffered a lot during the period of unrest prior to the 1914-18 War and its aftermath. It was also one

---

This chapter was originally published as 'The Eldonian Community in Liverpool' in *The Month*, July 1988, 784–90. I have expanded it to include more recent Eldonian initiatives and added a long postscript on inner-city parish reorganisation.

of the worst-affected areas during the bombing of Liverpool in the Second World War.

Post-war dispersal

After the war, in an attempt to cope with housing problems, many people were moved out of the area and were sent to newly-built overspill towns beyond the city boundaries. Although this meant that the local community was decimated, those who remained kept alive a deep sense of community. This had taken many generations to build up through sharing hard times together, through being good neighbours to each other and through the growth and intermingling of great family networks. Being a Catholic and belonging to the local parish was a taken-for-granted element of being a member of the local community. 'We're Our Lady's [or St Brigid's]' described where one came from as well as one's religious allegiance. This merging of parish and community identity was further consolidated by the parish school which all the children attended, and by the way Christian feasts and parish events often took the form of neighbourhood celebrations. In fact, those who had been moved out of the area envied those who had been left behind, since the new overspill towns lacked a sense of community and their very design often militated against any development of such a community consciousness.

The dislocation of people in the Vauxhall area was aggravated in 1968 by the building of the second Mersey Tunnel. This involved demolishing many of the tenements in the area and two of the local churches. Some of the residents were rehoused in the nearby Eldon Street neighbourhood. They in fact were the people who in 1978 provided the initial resistance to the next phase of demolishing the tenements in the area, feeling particularly threatened since at this time Liverpool City Council had no plans for any further house building. Hence this group realised that the community of people living in the tenements would be dispersed in all directions to wherever there might be vacant municipal housing. Having lost their homes once already without being allowed any part in the decision-making process and having seen how a long-established community can be destroyed by a thoughtless rehousing policy, these people were determined that they would not let the same thing happen again. By means of several major surveys they sounded out their neighbours to see whether they agreed with their 'staying put' policy. People were asked: did they want to move, or be rehoused locally, or stay in their flats or form housing co-operatives? No one had ever asked the local residents their views before. When the surveys were collated, a community housing policy was drawn up with the full consent of all concerned. A committee was formed to work for the implementation of this housing policy, and it was from this committee that eventually 'The Eldonians' came into being.

Eldonians against the Liverpool City Council

Their story is one of a long and hard struggle. They encountered bitter opposition from the Militant-dominated Liverpool City Council, who were determined to keep all housing decisions firmly in their own hands. They had their blueprint of urban regeneration for the whole city and they were not prepared to let it be disrupted by local people who were demanding a major say in what was going to happen to them. With the timely support of Archbishop Derek Worlock and Bishop David Sheppard at a key stage in the struggle, the Eldonians managed to safeguard the most important elements of their housing policy, even though some compromises had to be accepted.

Nevertheless, the bitter opposition they encountered and the struggle they went through together helped the Eldon Street neighbourhood to grow as a community. In no way was this the birth of an entirely new community spirit. It was more the flowering of a community spirit which already had deep roots in people's lives. Its real foundations had been laid over many generations and had been paid for by the shared sufferings and self-sacrifice of parents and grandparents over many years. It was the threat that their neighbourhood was about to be disbanded and destroyed by the City Council that gave a new lease of life to this deep sense of community. This was helped enormously by the fact that quite a few of the local people involved were richly endowed with leadership qualities, some to an outstanding degree. These men and women played an indispensable role in enabling the community to be actively involved in everything that was going on. As a consequence of this, life is no longer something that happens to them as a result of the decisions of some distant powers-that-be. Rather, life is largely determined by decisions in which they themselves play a major role, thus ensuring that the dignity of ordinary people living in the neighbourhood is properly respected.

The Eldonians and living the gospel

'Love your neighbour as yourself' lies at the heart of the gospel message. It is this same combination of neighbourly concern, self-confidence and self-respect which is so distinctive of the Eldonians. It is this which makes them a community which really fits the description 'Christian'. They have found tremendous strength in their togetherness, and this has enabled them to support each other in a most realistic and practical fashion.

The Eldonian Village

This support has been most evident in the field of housing. Their solidarity has completely changed their future as a community. If the City Council's plans had been allowed to go ahead, their tenements would have been demolished and they would have been dispersed to various parts of the city. The community would have been totally destroyed. Due to their courageous corporate opposition to the Council's action, this destruction was averted.

In the summer of 1988 the first Eldonians began moving into their homes in what they have chosen to call 'the Eldonian Village'. It is built on the site of the former Tate and Lyle factory which closed down in 1981 with the loss of employment for 2000 people, most of them from the surrounding area, among them many Eldonians. Consequently, families have been able to stay together in the same neighbourhood where their forebears had lived over many generations. The first phase of the

Eldonian Village, which was completed in 1989, comprised 145 houses. The second phase, finished in 1995, added a further 150 houses to the village. The houses in both phases were all designed with the involvement of those who were to live in them and were made up of family dwellings, bungalows and homes for people with special needs. Many of the tenants are young local families moving into a first home of their own. The Eldonians run the village along co-operative lines. This means that they are responsible for its general upkeep and repairs and for the allocation of housing within the village. The Eldonians have managed to achieve all this, and much else besides, through working in very close co-operation with a whole variety of organisations, most particularly with the Merseyside Development Corporation, the Housing Corporation, English Estates, Riverside Housing Association, the Co-operative Bank and the Liverpool Housing Trust. In recent years they have even developed a close working relationship with Liverpool City Council which is in striking contrast to the earlier situation during the Militant domination of the Council. The motto of the Eldonians 'We do it better together' applies not just to their mutual support for each other as neighbours in the one community. It also applies to their working with outside agencies. Their deep sense of self-respect and their determination that they have a right to the major say in decisions affecting their own lives, enables them to insist that their relationship with other agencies is always one of partnership and co-operation and never one of subservience or being second-class citizens.

Care in the Eldonian community

The Eldonians' strong sense of community and neighbourly concern has not been limited to the field of housing. One thing has led to another. Their concern has led them to look at the job situation in the area and also at health and environmental issues. The creation of Eldonian House, a purpose-built residential care home which caters for thirty residents, meets the care needs of frail elderly people in the locality, enabling them to stay within the community, close to family and friends. It also creates jobs and offers training for local people in residential care, and brings the added bonus that the residents are looked after by people they know and can trust, sometimes even members of their own families. Another very successful venture has been the Eldon Woods Day Nursery which provides fifty full-time places for babies from three months to pre-school entry children. Run as a partnership between the Eldonians and the Littlewoods Organisation, it caters for Littlewoods employees and, at a subsidised rate, for local residents. Once again, it creates jobs and offers professional training for local people. Another facility for the community is the Eldonian Village Hall. A popular venue for local social events and family and community celebrations, it is also helping to attract people from other parts of the city. In 1998 the Elaine Norris Sports Centre was opened in the Eldonian Village. This is adjacent to the bowling green and five-a-side football pitch cum tennis courts (both opened in 1997) and is a state-of-the-art indoor sports centre. Many of these ventures have been possible through close collaboration with the Merseyside Development Corporation. In all these exciting developments, the Eldonians have had to be 'learning on the job', one of the most effective forms of adult education. They have had to create the organisational structures as and when needed.

One such structure has been the Eldonian Development Trust. This is a good example of the Eldonian motto 'We do it better together'. In addition to the five of its directors drawn from the local community, the Development Trust has co-opted on to its board four prominent Liverpool business people to help with their professional expertise. Among its achievements the Trust can list the following: it has attracted public and private investment, it has co-ordinated public, private and community initiatives and it has also arranged retraining for some of the unemployed. With the backing of European Social Fund money it has also put on Personal Development courses in various parts of the neighbourhood to help local people get back to work. It is currently working on the possibility of developing a generation of community businesses, covering social and economic needs in the area, including the setting up of a building and maintenance company employing local people and tendering for local construction and maintenance contracts.

The Eldonians' environmental concern has been further in evidence in the major role they played in promoting creative thinking and planning to regenerate a large tract of land in the neighbourhood which had been left virtually derelict since the run-down of the north-end docks and the demise of much of the local industry. Once again they saw this as a co-operative venture between themselves and public and private bodies, including the Merseyside Task Force and the Merseyside Development Corporation. This 'north end' project is an example of the Eldonians' extending their activities beyond their own concerns and their immediate locality. Another example is the help they have given to other groups in the area who want to do something about their houses. In some cases the Eldonians have taken such groups under their wing as a community-based housing association. Their support of a group of harassed old-age pensioners living in some high-rise flats frequented by drug-users enabled these elderly people to move into co-operative housing of their own built on the site of the former St Gerard Majella Church. In other cases the Eldonians have given such groups practical help and support to make it possible for them to do something themselves, as was the case with the residents of St Aidan's Terrace in a neighbouring part of the city.

Living and growing

This outgoing dimension of the Eldonians' concern has developed naturally. As they have grown in confidence and competence in being able to tackle their own seemingly insoluble problems, they have automatically become a focus of interest and encouragement for other groups with similar problems. If any such groups approach them, the Eldonians have always been more than willing to help and to share their experience and increasing expertise with them. In catechetical terminology this could be described as the 'missionary' side of their activity. However, the Eldonians would not be happy with such a description since in no way would they see themselves as 'experts' or people with ready-made solutions.

Though the situation in their own part of Liverpool, once considered almost hopeless, is gradually changing for the better, the Eldonians are not content to rest on their laurels. They live in an area which has suffered from multiple deprivation over many years and many of whose members continue to be at the rough end of Government cut-backs in health provision and social security benefits. Simply to survive as a community in such a situation is a constant battle. The Eldonians do not believe in settling for mere survival. For them living as a community means growing as a community. For them a community is not fully alive if it is not constantly trying to become more aware of the many things, little and big, which need to be done if life in the neighbourhood is going to answer the real human needs of all who are living there. This requires continued effort and a lot of self-sacrifice on the part of many individuals. Nevertheless, the Eldonians know how to enjoy themselves. A joyless community is a pale shadow of what a human community should be. The Eldonians find fulfilment in bringing happiness into the lives of many people in the neighbourhood: this enables them to enjoy life themselves. Celebrations of one sort or another are a regular feature of life in the community.

What has all this to do with pastoral theology?

'Pastoral theology' is not a term that is part of the everyday vocabulary of the Eldonians. They are not concerned with the niceties of theological language. For them what really matters is growing together as a concerned and loving community. They will go to any lengths to resist injustice being done to themselves and their neighbours. They believe in the dignity of ordinary people like themselves and they will do all they can to help others realise their own dignity and to make sure it is respected, especially by those in public positions of responsibility. This is the vision of life they believe in and want to share with others. It is this attitude to life that they are trying to pass on to their young people by the living witness of their own committed lives. If other people want to use the term 'pastoral theology' to describe what it is they are involved in through this vision and commitment to living Christianity, the Eldonians will not object. However, they will object if it is suggested that their life and vision has nothing to do with their Christian faith since it is only about human community and human values.

For the Eldonians being a concerned and committed human being in one's own local community is what the Kingdom of God implies in everyday life. They would not want to claim that there is no more to the Kingdom of God than their own experience of community living; but they would want to resist any suggestion that living more fully as a human community is not a true, though incomplete, experience of the Kingdom of God in our world. For them, God becoming human in the person of Jesus truly is 'God with us'. The Eldonian motto 'We do it better together' can even be cashed theologically – 'we, God and humanity, do it better together'. That is even true of the suffering with us of God on the cross (God's com-passion). That gives the Eldonians hope and courage when they are faced with death, or tragedy or setbacks in the community. However, that is another story. . .

'Better together'

Although the Eldonians would not attach the label 'Catholic' to their neighbourhood organisation, they certainly draw inspiration from their Catholic faith. About twenty of them are at mass every day, some go each Sunday, many are not regular mass-attenders. However, virtually all of them would be at mass or at a sacramental celebration when the occasion is one of deep significance for the life of the local community. For instance, Our Lady's Church was packed to the doors when mass was an integral part of the community celebration of the beginning of the reclamation of the Tate and Lyle site. On this occasion the patronal feast of the parish (Our Lady of Reconciliation) and this important Eldonian event merged naturally together as one community celebration. It was also significant that this celebration was shared with many who were not Catholics. Taking part were Jews, Quakers, Anglicans and people from various other denominations. The ceremony of laying the first brick for the Eldonian Village was another celebration which drew people of different Churches and faiths together. David Sheppard, the Anglican Bishop of Liverpool, was the chief 'bricklayer' on that occasion, with Derek Worlock, the Catholic Archbishop, 'concelebrating'. It is worth noting that those two Church leaders went to the Eldonian motto for the title of a book which they co-authored. In a city once notorious for its own brand of Orange-Protestant versus Catholic hostility, *Better Together* is more than a catchy title for a book: it expresses both an achievement and a commitment. Even now when Derek Worlock has gone to his reward and David Sheppard has retired, the Eldonians keep their memory alive in the names of two streets in the village, Archbishop Worlock Close and Bishop Sheppard Court.

'We do it better together' expresses a profound truth about the life of the local community. For instance, the death of someone in the community is always an occasion of very deep human significance. There is no attempt to hide the awful reality of death. The dead person is laid out at home; all the neighbours come to visit the bereaved and to see the dead person for the last time. There is usually a large turn-out at the funeral mass at which an important feature of the liturgy is celebrating with the family the part the dead person has played in the life of the community. No one in the community would ever speak of a catechesis of death but every death in the community is a faith-event and a profound experience of the mystery of life.

New Eldonians

Birth too is as real as death in the Eldonian community. There are always plenty of babies around, more babies, in fact, than marriages. Birth, motherhood and fatherhood are not ideas to be talked about and analysed. The mystery-filled experience of giving birth to a child at the end of a mother's deeply personal involvement in her pregnancy is sometimes referred to in books as the mystery of 'co-creation with God'. Eldonian parents might say that it is simply a sign that their motto, 'We do it better together', is true of God as well! For them giving birth and being a mother or a father is part of what life is all about. These experiences certainly make them wonder about the meaning and origin of life and of themselves and about the immense responsibilities they have as parents. They realise that life is something much bigger than themselves and so they feel it is important to make something special of such an occasion as having a new baby. It does not come naturally to them to put what they are experiencing into abstract language but they feel a need to express, share and celebrate it with their family and friends and in the setting of their local community. Baptism enables them to do this. Their baby and their own experience is the very heart of this sacrament. In a sense, they do not need to be prepared for baptism: rather, the sacrament needs to be prepared for them. If the liturgy is to be properly sacramental (and therefore 'signifying', 'of significance'), the combination of symbols and words need to be such that the parents feel that the Church has enabled the birth of their new baby to be properly celebrated by the community. It is important that the wonder of their own life-giving experience is publicly acknowledged and is not passed by unnoticed and un-responded to. Consequently, it is the priest rather than the parents who needs to prepare for the baptism. He has to make sure that the baptism is fully efficacious (i.e. has its full effect) for the couple, their family and the community. The very least preparation he owes to the parents is to meet them beforehand and try to listen to what this new baby means as a faith-event in their lives. After all, the parents have experienced God in this event of their life together and the last thing they want the Church to do is to suggest that the God-experience is in the baptismal ceremony rather than in their own experience.

Involving the young

The Eldonians are deeply immersed in the everyday issues that affect their lives as human beings. It is this 'earthy' concern which makes them a real-life community and not just a discussion group about how to be a community. The Eldonians represent a very wide age-range. There are quite a few grandparents and even great grandparents among them. There are also young families. So children and young people feature largely in their concern. They are striving to involve their young people in everything they do. They recognise that the youth are their future. The starter and family houses that are part of the Eldonian Village are meant to encourage the young people to stay in the area. Without them the community could die out. This concern for the young people has led the Eldonians to play an active role as governors in the local schools and they make every effort to involve the schools in any community events that are taking place. They have also embarked on various schemes to provide sports and leisure facilities for the local young people since many of them have no job to go to when they leave school. During the building of the Eldonian Village, the Eldonians used their 'partnership' approach to get the building contractor to take on two local lads as apprentices. Moreover, as mentioned above, as part of their determination to secure employment for the young people in the area the Eldonians are involved in all sorts of initiatives and collaborative schemes to encourage investment and job creation in Liverpool. This practical concern for their young people is the way the Eldonians try to develop the self-respect and confidence of the youngsters in the neighbourhood. Without a sense of their own dignity as persons, the young people will not be able to take on board the vision and commitment of the Eldonians. It is hard for young people to believe that 'we do it better together' when they are unemployed. They can hardly be blamed for feeling that society is telling them, 'we do it better without you'!

Just as the term 'pastoral theology' is never used among the Eldonians, neither are they familiar with the notion of 'catechists' and 'catechetical programmes'. Some people may regard that as a deficiency and they may have a point. However, what certainly exists among the Eldonians are parents (especially mums), uncles and aunts, friends and neighbours, who are giving generously of their time and energy to make their community and their families somewhere where people are treated with respect and allowed to be themselves and live their own lives. Such generosity can rightly be called 'self-sacrifice' and seems to be directly in line with the invitation of Jesus to 'love one another as I have loved you', an invitation made on the very night he himself laid down his life for his friends.

The Eldonian ethos

All the above might seem too good to be true. While it is certainly true, it cannot be denied that there is a shadow side to every picture. The Eldonians have had their share of problems over the years. They have made their mistakes. There have been clashes of personality. As well as collaboration there has also been local rivalry, even touching on intolerance at times. Though it is essentially a community venture, the Eldonians benefited enormously from the gifted and strong leadership of some members of the community, most outstandingly Tony McGann. His inspired leadership has won him international recognition, as well as an MBE and an honorary doctorate from the University of Liverpool. But as we saw with Archbishop Worlock,[2] leading from the front exacts a heavy price from such a leader and can even tempt some of the community not to pull their weight.

The Eldonian Community would not claim that it is anywhere near perfect. It is made up of ordinary men and women, each with his or her own strengths and weaknesses. But they would claim that they are trying, however imperfectly, to be true to their motto. They really are struggling to do it better together and to live more and more as a community. That is where their commitment lies. It is this sense of commitment and their own example in trying to live up to it that they are hoping to pass on to their children. Those who speak in the language of 'catechetics' stress the paramount importance of 'ethos'. By 'ethos' they mean the atmosphere in any community, the real values which make a community what it really is. The 'Eldonian ethos' is profoundly human, profoundly Catholic, profoundly Christian. When such an ethos is present and when it has its influence on the local schools, perhaps the real 'catechist' is the community itself. This ties in with Christian belief about the presence and action of the Holy Spirit within people and within a community. The ethos (spirit) of the Eldonian community is the Holy Spirit acting powerfully in the people themselves. Maybe the real need for specialist 'catechists' and 'catechetical programmes' is where there is no real human, Catholic, Christian ethos (spirit) in a community. This raises a further question about the role of the Church itself.

The gospel is a message of reconciliation: reconciliation with God and reconciliation with each other. The Church in its role as 'sacrament of unity' must point beyond itself to where unity and reconciliation are actually being achieved. That is where the reality ('*res*') of the sacrament is. That is why the church of Our Lady's, Eldon Street, should point to the Eldonians as part of that reality. There is something profoundly Christian in their motto 'We do it better together'. It is a simple way of expressing the message of the Kingdom. To the extent that the Eldonians are able to live true to their motto and help their neighbours live in that way, to that extent God's Kingdom is present in this little corner of Liverpool. The original motto of the Eldonians, 'We do it better ourselves', was an initial statement of defiance against a Militant-dominated city council whose attitude was exposed in the words spoken to the Eldonians by one of its leaders: 'If we want your opinion, we'll give it to you'! However, the Eldonians soon came to see that their motto was not doing justice to the richness of their lived experience within the community and with those working in co-operation with them. 'We do it better together' was closer to the truth. It would be a tragedy if the priests of Our Lady's Church, Eldon Street, ever retreated from the theology implicit in the Eldonian motto by setting up parish programmes and activities which distracted the local people from their 'Kingdom work' of growing more closely together as a human community. This would be setting up the church in opposition to the Kingdom. The priests could even be accused of rank idolatry if they tried to suggest that the Kingdom was to be found in the church-going community rather than in the human community.

Postscript: Letter to an Archbishop: Some thoughts on parish reorganisation in the inner-city

One of the reasons which made me hesitant to accept the invitation to move from Our Lady's, Eldon Street, to St Basil and All Saints in Widnes was the fact that I felt there was a lot of unfinished business still on the agenda to do with the reorganisation of the church in inner-city Liverpool. Some of my anxieties are expressed in the following excerpts from a letter I wrote to Archbishop Kelly in May 1998:

> At one of our deanery meetings after he came as parish priest to Our Lady's, Peter Sibert made a very interesting and perceptive comment. He remarked on all the regeneration that had been taking place in the deanery, housing, environment, small industries, jobs, etc. He suggested that this would be the appropriate context in which any church reorganisation should be explored. In other words, when the area was going through a phase of regeneration in so many other ways, it was only natural that the church in the area should face its own need for regeneration. I thought that was a very important insight. Seen in that context, drawing people into exploring the needs of church reorganisation would not be seen as the equivalent of consulting people about their own funeral arrangements (i.e. feeling they are part of a dying church) but rather as the exciting challenge of church renewal and regeneration (i.e. resurrection).
>
> Of course, proposing such a context could be simply a cynical manipulation of people to gain approval for an already agreed programme of parish amalgamation and church demolition. That is the very opposite to what I am suggesting. That is why drawing on Peter's insight also demands looking seriously at what we should be about as church in the Vauxhall area. I do not think there is any simple answer to what it means to be the church in Vauxhall. That is because the church here has to cater for the needs of very disparate groups of people.
>
> There are the large numbers of middle-aged and elderly

people. Most people who attend church belong to this group. The church they attend is an important part of their personal identity. They look to the church as a centre of worship, devotion and prayer. In a changing and increasingly threatening society, they see the church as a secure base in their lives. This age-group also play a key role in sustaining some of the important inherited values which make communities in this part of Liverpool so rich and remarkable.

Then there are the men and women in the area who may not be church-going but who are deeply committed to improving living conditions in the area, especially for people who are socially deprived and in greatest need. Though not church-goers, they are sacrificing themselves for the values linked to social justice and human dignity and so are involved in a 'constitutive dimension of proclaiming the gospel', according to the 1986 Synod of Bishops. What these people need from the church is affirmation and practical support. They need a church which will give gospel meaning to the self-sacrificing other-centred activity they are involved in. They need a church which will help them celebrate their achievements and which will be with them in their frustrations, failures and set-backs. A church will only be able to do this if it is close to them, listening to their experiences, speaking a language they understand and using symbols which have meaning for them. At present, most of these people find little of these needs answered by the church. That is why they have drifted away and feel so alienated from the life and liturgy of the church.

Next there are the disaffected young people. Many of them have plenty of life about them, but find little meaning and inspiration in their lives. Peer pressures are enormous and are linked to the whole drug and alcohol scene. Traditional bases of authority, including the church, seem foreign to them and exert no appeal. I am at a loss as to how the church should respond to the needs of this group. I am certain that their spiritual needs are very profound and important and that they are somehow linked to questions of meaning in life and personal dignity and self-worth. I am equally certain that we are nowhere near responding to their needs.

The final group I want to mention is the children. In our deanery, Sunday mass is not part of the lives of most of our children. Why is this? Our instinctive reaction is to put the blame on their parents. Maybe we, as church, have to bear an even greater responsibility. Though children have a place in church and at the Eucharist, Christianity is not a childish religion. It is an adult faith. The church is not answering the deepest needs of children by drawing crowds of children to a specially adapted children's liturgy. It is far more important for the church to respond to the deepest needs of the parents of these children. The normal Sunday liturgy should not be a children's liturgy, nor a liturgy attended mainly by the elderly in the community. It should be a liturgy which relates to the lives of families. The church will not be able to offer such a liturgy if it is not in tune with the needs of the two groups mentioned in the two previous paragraphs.

I believe that any reorganisation of the church in our area which fails to begin from these basic questions about the meaning of being the church in Vauxhall and which is purely buildings-based and dictated by financial considerations linked to numbers attending Sunday mass will be an unmitigated disaster. As well as arousing tremendous opposition, it will merely strengthen the impression that the church is not really in touch with what local people are about. It will confirm the 'them and us' syndrome.

In saying this, I am in no way denying that the issue of church buildings needs to be addressed. Nor am I suggesting that the financial dimension is not a critical one that needs urgent consideration. But it will only make sense to people if it is put in the wider context of spiritual regeneration. That is the only way of shifting the focus of attention from buildings to the deeper needs of people. Only then is there a chance of people seeing the demolition of much-loved churches as a way forward to releasing funds for the more urgent priority of spiritual regeneration.

Theologically, it is people who constitute the church in a locality, not the church building. Hence, it is important to resist any suggestion that the demolition of a church building means the closure of a parish community (or its amalgamation into a neighbouring parish). Where there is a living parish community, we are in the presence of something sacred. A parish community is a sacramental entity. Certainly, it cannot be denied that sometimes a parish needs to be closed or amalgamated, if it can no longer function viably as a Christian community. Yet such closures or amalgamations need to be handled with extreme sensitivity and pastoral care. The withdrawal of a full-time priest or the financially necessary demolition of the church are not necessarily adequate criteria for closure or amalgamation. The closure or amalgamation of a parish community, if based on inadequate criteria, could on occasion be almost a sin against the Holy Spirit who is the very soul of the community.

At an away-day devoted to an initial exploration of the various issues related to church renewal in our part of the inner-city, one of the priorities established by the priests of the deanery was to work towards some kind of Deanery Assembly to explore how the church in the deanery could be regenerated and look at the practical implications of this in terms of clergy, buildings, lay formation, etc. It was agreed that for such an assembly to be effective, there would need to be genuine parish councils involving lay-people who were truly representative of the main areas of life in the community. We saw this as implementing the Hierarchy's commitment to collaborative ministry as spelt out in the document, *The Sign We Give*.

We soon agreed that a major priority would be the holding of some kind of major deanery get-together at which people from our different communities could look together at the problems and needs of the area from a church point of view. The people invited would not just be the church-goers. We also wanted to bring in people who were playing a major role in the various self-help and community development initiatives in the area – and there are many such initiatives, some of them quite outstanding and playing a major role in the life of the area. Moreover, because our area is predominantly

Catholic in population, a lot of the people involved in these initiatives are themselves Catholics, even though they may not be church-going.

As I said at the outset of this letter, one of my major misgivings at leaving Our Lady's is the fact that we, the priests of the deanery, have failed to take seriously the urgency of launching such a major review of the needs of pastoral reorganisation in Vauxhall. And I have to accept my share of responsibility for that failure. That is very much on my mind at present. Moreover, it cannot be long before you and your advisors turn your attention to the reorganisation of the church in the north end of the city, now that you seem to have completed a clustering of parishes in the south end. My hope is that, set in the context of the regeneration of the area and following a process which would involve the participation of the people of the area, such a reorganisation could really reinvigorate the local church and provide an integrating function in the regeneration already taking place in other aspects of life in Vauxhall. My fear is that the life and mission of the church in our area would be further diminished and marginalised, if the reorganisation was imposed by dictate from above without proper consultation and was based purely on criteria to do with buildings, finance and mass attendance.

Could I close by making a suggestion which has been hovering at the back of my mind while I have been writing this letter. In the light of everything I have written above, would one way forward be for you, as Archbishop, to call a special Council for the Regeneration of the Church in the North End of Liverpool. Such a council would obviously need a lot of prior preparation and a truly representative group of local people would need to be involved in this preparation. Part of the preparation would entail assembling all the material (theological, demographic, financial, etc. etc.) needed to highlight the major issues to be faced. It would probably be best to present this material in a variety of ways – e.g. in the form of a written paper, an audio-visual presentation, etc., so that it would be accessible to everyone in the area who wanted to be part of the process. It would also be essential that there be ecumenical representation at the Council and, equally important, in its preparation. I am thinking especially of people like Henry Corbett, Vicar of St Peter's, and his wife, Jane. They are both far more in touch with the life and concerns of the local people than are most of our own clergy, myself included. Such a Council might offer a sufficiently broad pastoral context for considering all the major issues, including such emotive issues as reorganising parish structures. It would also be a striking witness to our commitment to honour what you and the rest of the bishops have said about collaborative ministry in your document, *The Sign We Give*. I often quote a phrase from Michael Maher, Dean of Studies at Ushaw: 'Collaborative ministry is not a more effective way of doing things; it is a more authentic way of being church.' I think that is spot on.

A couple of weeks ago I had a letter from a canon in another diocese who is a former member of the bishop's council there. He was asking my views about a decision the diocese had made to close a parish which was a vibrant community, though not great in numbers, and to demolish the church. The local people who had contributed to the building and upkeep of the church were not even consulted. The comment was made that it was nothing to do with them. Such decisions were the sole concern of the diocesan trustees. When I spoke to him, I said that I could not advise him canonically. However, theologically and in terms of human justice, it seemed to me that, though the local people did not have a right of veto since wider issues of the common good were involved, at the very least they had every right to be consulted. In line with Michael Maher, I would say that for a diocese to take such an action without consulting the local people would be acting in contradiction to everything a diocese claims to be.

Though directed to the particular situation in the north end of inner-city Liverpool, many of the points made in my letter might be relevant to similar pastoral situations further afield.

3

Collaborative Ministry: A Pastoral Experience in Skelmersdale

During the Second World War 'collaboration' was a bad word. It meant helping the enemy. In the post-Vatican II Church 'collaboration' is far from being a pejorative term. It could even be described as an essential characteristic of the Church. We see ourselves as called to be a collaborative Church. By baptism we were all enrolled as collaborators. For prospective adult members of the Church, the Rite of Christian Initiation of Adults (RCIA) programme provides a process of gradual initiation into collaboration.

Literally the term 'collaborator' means co-worker, an expression used by Paul himself of those who shared with him in the work of spreading the good news. Vatican II is strong in its insistence that we are all co-workers in the Church. In fact, the very life of the Church consists in 'co-work'. Its prayer life finds its highest expression in liturgy which means the 'work of the people'. That is why participation in liturgy is given top priority in the Constitution on the Liturgy. Its teaching, preaching and prophetic role is recognised as one which is shared by the whole community. At the level of the governing function in the Church, the post-Vatican II terms which are now in common parlance are 'collegiality', 'co-responsibility' and 'subsidiarity'.

This is part of an article which first appeared in *The Way Supplement*, Summer 1986, 3-15, under the title 'Formation for Collaboration'. The text has been slightly altered to take account of later developments. I have used the other part of this article to form Chapter 5 of this book under the title 'Collaborative Ministry in the Exercise of Teaching Authority'.

These are all terms belonging to the collaboration stable.

Actions speak louder than words. The credibility test for whether the Church believes in collaboration is not found in its official statements. Rather it lies in the extent to which the Church's liturgy is truly participatory, its mission of teaching, preaching and prophecy takes full advantage of all the gifts of its members, and its leaders respect and actively promote collegiality, co-responsibility and subsidiarity in all levels of Church life. This credibility test can be applied internationally, nationally and locally.

Although structures are important and bad structures can seriously impede collaboration, collaboration is essentially an attitude of mind. Admittedly, the main evidence that such an attitude of mind actually exists will be seen in the practical organisation and life of the Church. It is also true that one's personal appreciation and understanding of what collaboration really means will only develop and deepen to the extent that one begins to live and work collaboratively. Nevertheless, there has to be a kind of inner conversion if the whole process is ever to start moving. This is part of the conversion called for by Vatican II.

The seeds of collaboration are already present in our Church and in our local communities. In some instances these seeds have already germinated and are producing much fruit. On balance, however, collaboration has hardly been a hallmark of the Roman Catholic Church in recent centuries. To a large extent formation for collaboration will involve re-formation of the Church itself. This needs to be a reformation of our attitude of mind and also of our structures, organisation and relationships. Both must necessarily go hand in hand. At its most basic level formation for collaboration is about this dual process.

My own most formative personal experience of collaborative ministry was in Skelmersdale New Town. In 1980 the priests and sisters involved in the Skelmersdale Team Ministry asked Archbishop Worlock to appoint me as their new Team Leader. A few years earlier a deliberate decision had been made to organise the church in Skelmersdale on a team ministry basis. Consequently, instead of three separate parishes there were seven smaller eucharistic communities. This was to fit in with the way the New Town had been designed as seven units grouped round the town centre rather like the spokes of a wheel round its central hub. Each community had its own Sunday Eucharist; in four of the communities this was celebrated in their primary school since only three communities had their own church building. The whole church in Skelmersdale was served by a team of four priests and six sisters but every community related in a special way to one particular priest and sister. The seven communities had a life of their own, yet they were all conscious that they belonged to the one church of Skelmersdale. Interaction and co-operation between the communities happened in various ways, helped by the weekly team meeting and by the regular meetings of the Skelmersdale Pastoral Council on which all communities had elected representatives. There was a remarkable spirit of collaborative ministry among the actively involved members of the different communities. Conflicts occurred, certainly, but the collaborative approach enabled these to be worked through and for the most part resolved. There is no doubt that, at the time, the Roman Catholic Church in Skelmersdale constituted a serious attempt at collaborative ministry. I hasten to disclaim any credit for this initiative. It was firmly in place when I went to Skelmersdale, thanks to the persevering commitment of priests, sisters and people through much pain and tears in the process of giving birth to this collaborative ministry. I had the great joy and privilege of sharing in this exciting undertaking over five years. I can honestly say that, although I had been involved in the training and formation of priests for the previous fifteen years, my five years in Skelmersdale were some of the most formative and educative in terms of my forty years as a priest.

Collaboration means working together. We can only work together if we have a common purpose in mind. That is why producing a 'mission statement' can be such an important process for those engaged in collaborative ministry. It is a policy statement formulated and agreed upon by people working together. I am convinced that some kind of agreement like this is crucial if collaborative ministry is to work effectively and with a reasonable level of personal satisfaction and mutual support for all involved.

As part of growing together, the whole Roman Catholic community in Skelmersdale was involved in looking at the kind of church they believed in and wanted to grow into. This was an important and helpful listening and sharing exercise. A lot came out of it. Most importantly, all agreed that they wanted to be a caring and sharing church – not just for themselves but for the whole town. They believed, too, that an essential element of their mission was to join in helping to make Skelmersdale itself a caring and sharing community.

Encouraged by this common mind, the priests and sisters of the team ministry undertook the service of formulating into a 'mission statement' what had come out of this listening and sharing exercise. They also felt it was important that they should commit themselves to the kind of ministry appropriate to the Skelmersdale church with its common mind and faced with the daunting problems of a new town with widespread unemployment. They felt this was especially important since changes in personnel were constantly occurring and so the team was in a continual state of re-formation. Such a 'mission statement' would be an invaluable instrument in the selection of new team members. Although new members would bring in their own gifts (and to that extent each would further enrich the 'mission statement'), any priest or sister who could not subscribe to the 'mission statement' would not fit in with the style of collaborative ministry in operation in the Skelmersdale church. When this 'mission statement' was drawn up, it was submitted to the Skelmersdale Pastoral Council for approval to make sure that it was faithful to the common mind which had emerged from the earlier listening and sharing exercise.

Every 'mission statement' will be unique since every situation in which ministry is exercised is unique. Nevertheless, every 'mission statement' must try to answer at least four basic questions: (1) What do we believe is the Church's mission? (2) What are the particular characteristics of our local situation in which the Church's mission has to be carried out? (3) Given this particular situation, what kind of local church do we need to be? (4) What are the implications of this for us as full-time ministers? The Skelmersdale 'mission statement' which follows shows how those involved in collaborative ministry in Skelmersdale in the early eighties tried to answer those questions.

The mission statement of the Skelmersdale Collaborative Team Ministry

1. Vision of the church's mission

> By her relationship with Christ, the church is a kind of sacrament or sign of intimate union with God and of the unity of all humankind. She is also an instrument for the achievement of such union and unity. (*Lumen Gentium*, n. 1)

As a team we commit ourselves to the vision of the Church's mission as found in this statement from the Second Vatican Council. The Church is called to be a sign which points to the good news that God loves every man, woman and child on this earth and that we are all truly one family. With *Gaudium et Spes* (n. 40) we also believe that the Church shows this love particularly by her sharing in the work of restoring human dignity, strengthening the bonds of society and giving a deeper significance to people's everyday activities. Thus, the Church's very existence is in and for the world, created and loved by God our Father. The Skelmersdale church shares that mission but has to live it out in the specific context of Skelmersdale.

2. The particular characteristics of the local situation

Skelmersdale New Town has a population of some 43,000 people. They have the same needs and aspirations as other men and women throughout the country. In addition, Skelmersdale has its own particular features of life and these give rise to special needs and hopes.

(a) Negative characteristics

The title of a report commissioned by the local council puts very succinctly the reality of life for many people in the town, *Skem*

– *the broken promise*. Many individuals and families who came to Skelmersdale drawn by the promise of employment and a better quality of life had their hopes dashed by the failure of industry to expand as first envisaged. The above-mentioned report states: 'On those estates which were specifically built as New Town development, there is an unemployment rate which is above 32 per cent overall, with an even higher rate among males...In the worst affected area (Digmoor and Moorside) unemployment is running at about 35 per cent overall, with a male rate of almost 43 per cent.'[1] As a consequence, there is bitterness, loss of self-confidence and a sense of direction, and also an experience of powerlessness for many people in the community. Inevitably, family life is put under severe strain in such a situation and the impact on young people is a special cause for concern. High youth unemployment is a factor which causes many young people to seek to establish their adult status through parenthood and/or independent living, for both of which they are unprepared. Living under these kind of pressures can easily leave people depressed and apathetic. As *Skem – the broken promise* notes, all that can create a potentially explosive situation. Naturally, this is not the whole picture of Skelmersdale. Not everyone is unemployed. There are plenty of people living comfortably in the town and there are even areas of relative prosperity. Probably, some Skelmersdale people have no direct experience of the harder side of life in the town and would not recognise the picture just painted.

(b) Positive characteristics

Moreover, there is a very hopeful side to life in Skelmersdale. In a report prepared for the Liverpool Archdiocesan Pastoral Council the local church community spelt out its grounds for optimism. A great deal of effort is directed to community building activities. On the part of many groups and individuals in the town there is a very deep commitment to working to improve the quality of life in Skelmersdale. In the local communities there is a real sense of caring and, at times, a very tangible experience of being cared for. There is a spirit of openness, humour and resilience among people. While many of the people who have come to Skelmersdale from Liverpool maintain their links with family and friends in the city, they have no desire to move back there. Skelmersdale is now their home. These are all positive human features which help to explain why for many people Skelmersdale is a good place in which to live.

3. In this particular situation, what kind of local church do we need to be?

In the light of the above the church in Skelmersdale has a double task. It has itself to grow as a community. And it has also to work for the growth of the whole of Skelmersdale as a community. Its own members need to feel they are part of a loving and caring community. After all, they belong to the Skelmersdale context and share the same needs as everyone else. But from the basis of their own loving and caring community they must be empowered to work to make a loving and caring community within Skelmersdale itself and its different neighbourhood units.

(a) First part of double task: for the church itself to grow as a community

As a faith community believing in God's love for us and for all people, the church draws its inspiration and dynamism from this belief. That is why gathering together to celebrate God's love in its different manifestations in life is so crucial to the life of the church community. The Sunday Eucharist is not a distraction or an escape from life. Rather it renews and confirms the community in its commitment to be fully part of life and to help to transform that life in conformity with the dignity of people so precious in the eyes of God.

In the light of all the above the life of the church in Skelmersdale has its own unique character.

Quite deliberately it is not divided into separate parishes. It is a town-church with seven small eucharistic communities. In this way it is hoped that real community building can be facilitated in the different geographical areas of Skelmersdale, each with its own special character. At the same time the unity of purpose of the church's mission in the town can be preserved.

Being true to the special Skelmersdale context also commits us to a particular style of church life. Pastorally our approach must be such that it affirms and empowers people and we must avail ourselves of every opportunity for this. We are deeply committed to the development of lay leaders and lay ministries and to searching together for appropriate ways of education and formation. We are fully committed to our Skelmersdale Pastoral Council as an important means for communication, co-operation, consultation and sharing responsibility within and between our local eucharistic communities and in the town-church as a whole; and we will support any move to make the Pastoral Council a more effective means for these ends.

Being at the heart of our community life our liturgical celebrations must be real celebrations and must communicate and kindle the hope, comfort and power of the risen Lord and his total concern for our human life here in Skelmersdale today. The fact that our eucharistic communities are not very large and the people have more chance of knowing and caring for each other enables our liturgical celebrations to be more personal and better rooted in people's lives. This is something we treasure.

(b) Second part of double task: to work for the growth of the whole of Skelmersdale as a community

We accept, too, the need for both the individual and the church community as a whole to live out the mission to the town community. Naturally, this mission is also similarly shaped by the realities of our special Skelmersdale situation.

As a team we commit ourselves to continue to develop our own awareness and sensitivity to the major problems of our town.[2] We accept that this means we must strive to promote and encourage the involvement of our church in working for whatever changes are needed to bring about a satisfactory human solution to these problems. It further demands that we support those agencies and initiatives which seek to empower those who have little or no access to decision-making in areas affecting their own life decisions.

4. Implications for those working as full-time ministers

We recognise too that a further characteristic of our mission is that it is one which we share with other churches in the town. Therefore, as far as possible, we must carry out this mission ecumenically.

An important feature of the special character of the church in Skelmersdale is team ministry, with a team currently composed of four priests and five sisters.

The team approach to ministry provides support, encouragement and the opportunity for sharing vision and concern on a town-wide basis. It enables discussion and planning of common work which can then be interpreted and implemented at local level. It also allows for a broader look at possible responses both at team and local level to issues in Skelmersdale. Moreover, it allows for the strengths, gifts and expertise of the individual team members to be shared by the whole church in Skelmersdale.

Inevitably there are some disadvantages and tensions in team ministry which need to be acknowledged. Decisions may take longer to arrive at. There may perhaps be less personal autonomy than would be the case in a more conventional parish structure. The priests may feel an inner tension through the fact that the mutual support they give each other through living together (on the very edge of the town) is offset by their being less available in their local communities and by their not sharing the lifestyle of their own people.

In spite of these disadvantages (and the last-mentioned does not pertain to the essence of team ministry), team ministry has much to commend it. We believe it is an appropriate form of ministry for Skelmersdale. We need to look at ways in which it could develop in the future. In the light of a resolution from the Ministry Sector to the Liverpool Archdiocesan Pastoral Council in 1985, one possible development might be the inclusion on the team of more lay members who might well have special areas of expertise or responsibility, e.g. catechetics, education, finance, etc.

Conclusion

In recent years there has been a complete change of personnel on the team ministry and a major reduction in numbers. I suspect that the style of ministry has changed in the wake of this new situation. I hope it is still true to the fundamentals of collaborative ministry since it was the people themselves who gave birth to that. They took great pride in being a church trying to renew itself creatively in line with Vatican II.

Formation for collaboration is about re-forming our attitude of mind in the church. One characteristic of this collaborative attitude of mind stands out to me as being of paramount importance: *respectful and attentive listening in order to empower people to accept fully their own worth and share their gifts for the benefit of all.*

Collaboration is impossible among people who will not listen or who seek to dominate others by their power. Tragically, such attitudes are not uncommon in the Church. Collaborative ministry calls for much more than a change of style in ministry: it is an invitation to be more authentically church.

PART 2

Creative Tensions in Pastoral Ministry

4

Pastoral Care and Church Law: 'Mind the Gap'

As in Jesus' day, the life-giving wisdom of good laws continues to be at the service of pastoral ministry today. However, even good laws need to be handled well. What better law than the Sabbath – yet even that was open to abuse. Much of the art of pastoral ministry lies in interpreting good laws in such a way that they are life-giving for those for whom they are made. That is where the virtue of pastoral sensitivity comes in. Pastoral sensitivity is a mind-set rather than a set of rules of practice. The good pastoral minister is rather like the good artist: he or she needs to know the basic skills of the trade and the rules of thumb to be followed. However, more than that is needed. Like Jesus, the Good Pastor, a pastoral minister's main concern must be the needs of those under his or her care. Each of these people is a unique human person, situated at this unrepeatable moment in his or her personal story. What is good pastoral care for one person need not necessarily be so for another.

A resolution passed by the 1995 National Conference of Priests spoke of 'the growing gap between the official regulations of the Church and the demands of pastoral practice'. Such a gap is almost inevitable. After all, the philosophy of law embraced by the Church down through the centuries has always recognised that laws, because of their universality, have at best only general validity ('ut in pluribus', as Aquinas puts it,

---

In this chapter I have combined a working paper for the 1996 National Conference of Priests with part of a background reflection for a study session for members of the Bishops' Conference of England and Wales.

following Aristotle). That means that pastoral ministers need to develop the ability to discern when the good purposes of any law would be vitiated by keeping to the strict letter of the law in a particular instance. The traditional name for this ability is *epikeia,* which Aquinas insists is a virtue. It is part of the general virtue of justice. It is not an anarchic way of evading the law but its aim is, in fact, to make sure that the deepest purpose of the law is achieved. This will always be the pastoral good of persons in some form or other. That explains the wise dictum taught to priests in the seminary, 'salus animarum suprema lex' ('the salvation of souls is the law above all laws')! In the light of the National Conference of Priests' resolution *epikeia* could perhaps be called 'the gap virtue'. It is a virtue which is particularly important for all engaged in pastoral ministry. Moreover, it becomes increasingly important the greater the gap grows between the official regulations of the Church and the demands of pastoral practice.

It is sometimes suggested that for the sake of the common good laws should always be strictly observed. In fact, our tradition says the very opposite. The good of individual persons is an essential component of the common good. Hence, it is the common good itself which calls for the virtue of *epikeia.* Perhaps Jesus was making a similar point in his pastoral story about the shepherd leaving the ninety-nine and going to search for the lost sheep.

This gap virtue is needed right across the board in pastoral ministry. To explore what it might mean in practice, it might be helpful to look at one specific sphere of pastoral ministry, namely liturgy. Like all other Church laws, liturgical laws and rubrics need to be interpreted in a way which is pastorally beneficial to the people of God.

According to Vatican II 'the full and active participation by all the people is the aim to be considered before all else; for it is the primary and indispensable source from which the faithful are to derive the true Christian spirit' (*Constitution on the Sacred Liturgy*, n. 14). That is where the common good lies in the area of liturgy. The Liturgy Constitution and subsequent documents lay down liturgical regulations spelling out how this is to be achieved in practice. However, these regulations remain subservient to this fundamental principle spelt out in n.14. That is even true of the Constitution's general norm set out in n. 22: 'Absolutely no other person, not even a priest, may add, remove, or change anything in the liturgy on his own authority.' That is a wise and important regulation. Priests, badly instructed in the liturgy, can cause havoc, hindering the full and active participation of a congregation. Wisely, only a few lines after stating its basic principle, the Constitution insists that it is 'vitally necessary' that a high priority should be given to the liturgical instruction of the clergy. This is because a major part of the pastoral ministry of priests is to foster the full and active participation of the congregation in the liturgy.

However, liturgical instruction is essential but not sufficient. Complying with liturgical regulations does not guarantee good liturgy. Participation must not be simply a matter of ensuring that people are given the opportunity to take on active roles in a liturgical celebration. People must feel that liturgy touches their down-to-earth everyday experience at its inner core and gives expression to its deepest meaning. If, at times, this can only or best be achieved through creative and imaginative adaptation within the overall structure of the liturgy, that kind of flexibility is completely faithful to the fundamental principle of good liturgy. Priests who take such steps to facilitate the possibility of that depth of participation are merely exercising the gap virtue in their liturgical ministry. Of course, this would be impossible without a feel for the life-situations of the people in the congregation. That means that those responsible for the liturgy need to be closely in touch with the everyday lives of people. Elite liturgical teams, however well intentioned and liturgically literate, can wreak havoc in a parish if they are not in tune with the reality of the lives of people in the congregation. Moreover, it goes without saying that what is needed to achieve full and active participation will vary according to people's pastoral needs.

It might help to offer some specific examples from my own pastoral ministry in inner-city Liverpool. Life in Vauxhall is hard for most people. The negative effects of multiple deprivation over many generations are all too obvious. That is why pastoral practice has to take people where they are. Only in this way can it help them believe they are loved by God precisely 'where they are'. In the eyes of God they are precious people, not just statistics in a table of social deprivation. It is belief in their own dignity which provides the springboard for further growth. This belief in themselves is being strengthened by their experience of being able to improve some of the social conditions affecting their lives. Sound pastoral practice must consolidate that experience. Therefore, the main thrust of pastoral ministry in such a situation is to help people feel that everything that they experience as good in their lives is accepted, affirmed and celebrated in the presence of God. The priests in the area are not in the business of judgement and condemnation. Where their people are at is different from a middle-class parish. Though most of them are not regular church-goers, in no way should they be labelled as 'non-practising Catholics'. They really do 'practise' their faith in the gospel sense of struggling to do their best to live lives of justice and love, often in situations where the odds can seem stacked against them. 'I belong to Our Lady's' is usually part of how they would describe themselves. It would be appalling pastoral practice for a priest to contradict or undermine this belief and pride in their Catholic identity. Hence, the message they hear in the liturgy should not be a disheartening 'no' condemning them where they are presently at in their lives. Rather it needs to be a resounding 'yes', accepting them where they are at but also encouraging them to believe that they are capable of even greater things. They need to be empowered to hear the gospel as 'Good News' in their lives. If the liturgy is, as the Liturgy Constitution insists, a 'primary and indispensable source' from which they derive the true Christian spirit of this Good News, then doing whatever is needed to help them to participate fully and actively in the Eucharist is a serious responsibility on those who serve as pastoral ministers in the community.

Against that background, I believe that I and my fellow priests were exercising the gap virtue (and, at the same time, respecting the fundamental principle of liturgy) when we held general absolution services in Advent and Lent or incorporated a short penitential rite with general absolution in any Eucharist where there was a fair number of 'non regular church-goers' from the local community in the congregation. Sometimes we used 'home-made' eucharistic prayers which fitted in with the Sunday readings or the particular feast being celebrated or special occasions in the lives of those sharing in the Eucharist. With couples cohabiting or in a second marriage after divorce or who habitually missed Sunday mass, we normally raised no objections to their having their children baptised. And when, in the strange ways of God's providence, they were drawn to come to the Eucharist we were happy if they felt at peace in their conscience to come forward to receive Communion.

These are not offered as examples of recommended pastoral practice which others ought to adopt. Different local situations require different pastoral solutions. For some these examples may be very unacceptable. In fact, whether any or all of these practices can be adequately justified in pastoral theology is not the point. The point is that 'the demands of pastoral practice' must always come first if we are to minister pastorally after the model of Christ himself. The old dictum, *salus animarum suprema lex*, could be translated as 'where there is a gap between the official regulations of the Church and the demands of pastoral practice, the latter must always take priority'. Of course, obedience has a place in pastoral ministry. Pastoral ministers are not commissioned 'to do their own thing'. But obedience (*ob-audire*) is about listening. The ears of the good shepherd will always be alert to hear the cries of the sheep. Listening to people's deepest needs and discerning how best to respond to them is one of the main ways a pastoral minister hears and obeys the voice of God. Whatever else the call to holiness in pastoral ministry is about, it is certainly about that. Holiness and pastoral life cannot be put in separate compartments.

How does this kind of pastoral practice fit in with a pastoral minister's duty to live in communion with his or her local bishop and with the wider Church? Is it not bound to provoke a reaction from the bishop? The impression is sometimes given that the 'communion' bishops should be concerned about is a negative kind of communion, namely, making sure that nothing is done to rock the boat or provoke criticism from the Vatican. Wanting to be sympathetic towards the kind of 'divergent' pastoral practices mentioned above, a bishop who feels constrained by his concern for that negative kind of communion might feel that the best support he could give would be to turn a blind eye to what is happening at parish level. Clearly, that kind of 'I would rather not know what you are doing' stance is far preferable to outright prohibition. Nevertheless, it is not entirely satisfactory from the point of view of pastoral theology. After all, the pastoral practices mentioned above and those similar to them are actually about living and deepening communion at local level. It is that positive communion of life that a bishop, as pastor, is primarily called to serve. Provided the practices in question are solidly based in sound pastoral theology (and that assessment would need a sensitive appreciation of the locality and its people), they are precisely the kind of thing bishops should be encouraging in their role as servants of communion. The main focus of a bishop as servant of communion should not be on seeing that the letter of the law is observed. It should be on seeing that the deepest gospel values (of which laws are servants, not masters) are being honoured in pastoral practice.

5

Collaborative Ministry in the Exercise of Teaching Authority

Collaboration should be operative in every facet of the Church's life and mission. In Chapter 3 I shared my experience of collaborative ministry at a pastoral level in the innovative team ministry parochial situation in Skelmersdale New Town. In this chapter I would like to explore what collaborative ministry should mean for the life of the universal Church and particularly with regard to its mission of teaching and evangelisation.

The Church's mission of teaching and evangelisation is essentially a collaborative mission. When we talk about 'teaching', we naturally think of someone called the 'teacher' passing on knowledge, information or skills to other people called the 'pupils' or 'learners'. The word 'teacher' focuses on what the teacher is doing. It makes his activity the major ingredient in what is happening. If a teacher knows his material and puts it over clearly, then the responsibility rests with the pupils if they fail to learn.

For much of my time teaching moral theology in the seminary that is how I thought of teaching. I taught; my pupils were taught. However, some years ago, as a result of a course on the processes of adult learning, I underwent a kind of Copernican revolution in my understanding of my role as a teacher. I came to realise that I was working within the wrong frame of reference. The principal frame of reference is not

---

This chapter comprises part of an article 'Formation for Collaboration', which was originally published in *The Way Supplement*, Summer 1986, pp. 3-15.

'teaching', but 'learning'. Our main concentration must be on the learning process. If no learning occurs, no real teaching is taking place, however well teachers might think they are teaching and however excellent their material might be objectively speaking. A firm grasp of this point is crucial if we are to understand the Church's mission to teach (and evangelise) as essentially a collaborative venture.

The Church is not a community divided into two groups, the teachers (the pope and the bishops) and those who are taught (the rest of us). That kind of presentation was a nineteenth-century innovation and went very much against the more traditional and biblical notion which saw 'learning' and 'teaching' as two activities involving the whole Church. As Christians we are all learners and as Christians we are also all teachers. Unpacking that statement might help us to appreciate the collaborative nature of Christian teaching.

As Christians we are all learners.

This immediately calls to mind the words of Jesus, 'You must not allow yourselves to be called teachers, for you have only one teacher, the Christ' (Matt. 23:10). As believers we are all equally dependent on the Lord for the gift of faith, be we pope or peasant. At this level we are all equal. In fact, at this level, strange though it might sound, we all share equally in the charism of infallibility. This is the infallibility of the Church in believing.[1]

There is a certain dynamic element at work in any group gathered together to share in a learning experience. In the Church it is the Holy Spirit who is the dynamic element in the learning process. That is why the Church needs to have a basic trust and confidence in its internal learning process and should allow it to take its natural course.

The heart of this learning process does not lie in the passing on of correct teaching from one generation to the next. Revelation is not a block of objective knowledge which was committed to the apostles by Jesus and which is passed down from age to age. Bishop Butler remarks that 'a revelation is not fully given until it is received'.[2] In other words revelation is a living reality which occurs in every generation in the sense that the process of self-discovery in Christ has to be worked through by the Church in every age and in each culture.[3] The Word of God being received and appropriated in each generation is the living process of revelation.

As Christians we are all teachers.
There is a sense in which that is true within the learning community of the Church. We all share our faith with each other and thus help on the growth process in the body of the Church – parents, teachers and catechists doing this in a very crucial way.

By virtue of our baptism we also share in the missionary function of the Church. 'Go and teach all nations' is a word of the Lord spoken to all of us. This is put forward very forcefully by Paul VI in his Apostolic Letter, *Evangelization in the modern world*, following the 1974 Synod of Bishops. He writes: 'Here lies the test of truth, the touchstone of evangelization: it is unthinkable that a person should accept the Word and give himself to the kingdom without becoming a person who bears witness to it and proclaims it in his turn' (n. 24). In this letter the Pope seems to opt for the learning frame of reference rather than the teaching one. 'In fact, the proclamation only reaches full development when it is listened to, accepted and assimilated, and when it arouses a genuine adherence in the one who has thus received it' (n. 23). Therefore, in our role as teachers, as evangelisers, we need to be very aware that the core of evangelisation does not lie in what we do but rather in what happens in the hearts and minds of those with whom we are trying to share the gospel. We are not defending the gospel against the enemy; we are sharing it with people who deep down in their being are hungry for the word of God.

Where does the teaching authority of the pope and the bishops fit into all this? Again it depends on whether one adopts the teaching frame of reference or the learning one. If one goes for the former, both the pope and the bishops are thrust into an impossible position. To be competent teachers they would need to be mini-universities embodying in themselves all the expertise of theological, biblical, moral, philosophical, pastoral and historical disciplines. That kind of teaching competence would be humanly impossible. However, it is completely different if learning is accepted as the prime process. Then teaching is seen as a leadership role within (not outside) the learning process. The teachers remain one hundred per cent a member of the learning community but their function is to facilitate the learning process within the community. Let us try to explore what are the main functions of teaching authority within the Church if it is interpreted according to the learning frame of reference?

First of all, a 'learning' teaching authority will be conscious that ultimately there is one teacher in the Christian community and that is the Holy Spirit, the life-giving Spirit of truth which Christ has breathed into his Church. This Spirit permeates the whole Church and so teachers, whether they be pope, bishop or head of the Congregation for the Doctrine of the Faith, should not see themselves as the repository of all wisdom and knowledge or as having some kind of 'hot-line' to God. They will see themselves very much as listeners, trying to discern all the riches of the Spirit's wisdom coming through different members of the community. And when they discern the voice of the Spirit, coming from whatever quarter, they will see it as part of their role to enable that voice to be heard as widely as possible in the Church.

Secondly, a 'learning' teaching authority today will be open to the riches of the Church's self-understanding as articulated in Vatican II and so will be conscious that the Spirit-guided learning community must not be restricted to the Roman Catholic Church. Speaking of non-Catholic Christians, *Lumen Gentium* (n. 15) says that 'to them also the Holy Spirit gives his gifts and graces and is therefore operative among them with his sanctifying power.'[4] And implicit in Vatican II's *Declaration on the relationship of the church to non-Christian religions* is the truth that, even outside the gathering of Christian believers, the learning process is going on and the Spirit of God is active. Moreover, speaking of the whole movement among peoples directed towards promoting deeper respect for the human person, *Gaudium et Spes* (n. 26) comments: 'God's Spirit, who with a marvellous providence directs the unfolding of time and renews the face of the earth, is present in this evolutionary process'. (The phrase 'is not absent from' in the Abbot translation does not do justice to 'adest' in the Latin text.[5]) So if the Church is to exercise a teaching function in the world, it must first play a listening role since in every age and culture the heart of revelation must be clothed in the best riches of the world's true self-understanding.[6]

A third element in the role of the 'learning' teaching authority is the willingness to join in dialogue. Dialogue is an essential part of teaching according to the learning model. It is a dialogue partly directed towards listening and learning and partly towards sharing one's own beliefs and convictions. Dialogical teaching does not need to claim certainty for all its utterances. There can be a danger in the Church of thinking that all pronouncements by teaching authority ought really to be infallible or at least one hundred per cent certain! Since pronouncements relevant to current issues can hardly be infallible, the Church is forced into a catch-22 situation – either it keeps a deafening silence or else it claims a level of authority for its statements which they will not bear. This need not be the case if a teaching pronouncement is offered as a dialogical contribution within the learning community. A strong, well-presented and carefully agreed statement which tries to express as well as possible Christian thinking on a current issue can play an important role in the dynamic of the learning community. The two Pastoral Letters of the United States' bishops, 'The Challenge of Peace: God's Promise and Our Response' (1983) and 'Economic Justice for All: Catholic Social Teaching and the U.S. Economy' (1986) are striking examples of this dynamic both in the painstaking public consultation process involved in their composition and in their self-description as a contribution to an ongoing dialogue.[7]

A fourth element in the role of the 'learning' teaching authority in the Church will be the function of articulating the community's grasp of the truth when this has emerged with sufficient clarity and agreement. This, too, demands attentive listening and careful discernment. Part of this listening and discernment will be directed towards earlier teaching. In saying this I am not suggesting that teaching cannot develop or even change. There is no denying the possibility of development of doctrine or even of change of teaching when we have outgrown mistaken notions in certain matters related to the truths of Christian faith. This has happened, for example, with regard to some aspects of our understanding of human sexuality with the consequence that the teaching of Vatican II shows a definite change from the teaching of the patristic age and succeeding centuries. Nevertheless, we cannot deny our past. If our teaching has developed or even changed, this must be acknowledged and the reasons for it must be understood. We are unfaithful to Christian tradition if we refuse to accept the possibility of development or change. Christian tradition is something alive and active. Healthy development and change is collaboration with our Christian forebears, since it is keeping alive the tradition they handed on to us.

Would it be fair to say that a fifth element in the role of teaching authority is the function of prophet? If by prophecy we mean a special gift of being able to interpret the signs of the times, I would not link that necessarily with the role of the teacher, even though I would gladly admit that many teachers in the Church have exercised this prophetic gift. I would prefer to say that part of the teacher's role is to listen for the voice of the prophet and then enable that voice to be heard as widely as possible. The calling of Vatican II by Pope John XXIII was a classic example of this. Perhaps John XXIII was not a prophet himself but by calling the Council he enabled the voices of some of the great prophets of our day to echo round the whole Church – and far beyond as well. I would even dare to say that John XXIII's summoning of the world's bishops together for the Second Vatican Council (accompanied by their theological consultors) was the most important exercise of teaching authority this century.

What about dissent from authoritative teaching in the Church? Provided it is not touching the heart of our Christian faith and so dealing with truths believed and taught infallibly, there is room for dissent. Even here of course, the way we interpret dissent will depend on whether we are thinking within the teaching or the learning frame of reference. In the teaching model, dissent is seen as a rejection of the teaching put forward – 'You, the teacher, are wrong. You are in error'. Understood in this way dissent usually involves confrontation between teacher and taught. Nevertheless, traditional theology allows for such dissent in exceptional circumstances, though it was thought that it would only happen rarely. In the learning model, dissent is not a confrontation with the teacher. It is much more an expression of collaboration in the Church's teaching. It is claiming that the articulation of this teaching put forward by the teacher does not do justice to the full riches of what the Church really believes. A good indication as to whether a particular act of dissent is justified will be found in the reaction of the rest of the community, especially those most intimately involved in that specific issue, whether as practitioners or as teachers. That is why the 'non-reception' of some of the Church's teaching on sexual and marital issues cannot be dismissed too easily. As Cardinal Hume said at the 1980 Synod of Bishops, the experience of Christian married couples is a genuine source for the Church's exploration of the theology of marriage.

Collaboration in the Church's mission of teaching and evangelisation is a privilege and responsibility of us all. The Church will be truly honouring collaboration in this aspect of its mission when the voice of the Spirit is heard and listened to, through whomsoever it speaks and from whatever unlikely quarter it might come.

6

Co-responsibility and Accountability within a Sinful Church

Each time we assemble as church to celebrate Eucharist we begin by acknowledging our need for forgiveness; and we go on to prepare to share in Holy Communion by making a common declaration: 'Lord, I am not worthy...'. Since Vatican II tells us that 'the real nature of the true Church' is revealed in the liturgy (cf. *Constitution on the Sacred Liturgy*, n. 2), it is clear that we are committed to a belief that we are a Church of sinners.

To say that we believe in a Church of sinners can be understood in a very weak sense, i.e. it is within a Church of sinners that we believe. This would be saying no more than that the Church, though holy in itself, is made up of members who individually are more or less sinful. This would imply that the holiness of the Church is not affected by the sinfulness of its members. It exists on a higher plane beyond the reach of our personal sinfulness. In his two essays, 'The Church of Sinners' and 'The Sinful Church in the Decrees of Vatican II',[1] Karl Rahner reminds us that such a view is contrary to Catholic belief. There is no metaphysical Church which has an existence of its own, separate from the flesh and blood men and women who are its members. We, the members of the Church, actually are the Church. Our sins are sins of the Church. They do not merely weaken the Church's witness to God's call to universal holiness. Through us, the Church is actually the subject of sin.

This is a revised version of my article 'Do we believe in a Church of Sinners?', which originally appeared in *The Way*, 1993, 106-16. For a somewhat similar approach from a moral theologian writing from within the Irish context, cf. Raphael Gallagher, 'In the Noise of War the Word Got Lost', in *The Furrow*, 1997, 391-8, especially 395-6.

Some Christians might feel uneasy with such a stark attribution of sinfulness to the Church and might be tempted to tone it down a little. After all, the Creed professes belief in a Church which is 'holy', not 'sinful'. Would it not be sufficient to admit that this 'holy' Church is, in its historical existence, defiled by the sins of its members but that, when the overall picture is seen, it is the holiness of the Church that predominates, not the sinfulness of its members?

Such a position is too complacent about the sins of the members of the Church. Christians who sin sin as Christians. If, to use Paul's metaphor, Christians are members of the body of Christ, Christians who sin make the body of Christ the subject of sin. If that is so, surely it is horrendous. For Paul the horror of it is vividly expressed in the question he poses to the church in Corinth: 'Do you think I can take parts of Christ's body and join them to the body of a prostitute?' (1 Cor. 6:15)

In the course of history some Christians have tried to evade this whole issue by claiming that sinners do not really belong to the Church. They are only nominal Christians. In reality, their sin has either put them outside the Church or else has shown them up as never really belonging to the true Church. Movements for Church reform down through the centuries have often been tempted to adopt this position. In its wisdom the Church has always recognised that it is contrary to our gospel-based faith to say that sinners do not belong to the Church.

This is a very salutary reaction. It means that the Church cannot be excused from tackling its own sinfulness. The sinfulness of the Church is a reality that cannot be denied. It is also a tragedy. The question every Christian has to face, if he or she really believes in the Church, is 'how am I to respond to the sinfulness of the Church I believe in? What am I going to do about it?' An obvious answer to that question is 'Physician, heal yourself'. In other words, as we shall see in Chapter 11, each of us has to face up to his or her own sinfulness, since that is my own personal contribution to the sinfulness of the Church. Nevertheless, our concern must look beyond our own sinfulness. The Church is more than a collection of individual Christians.

Sinner – an ambiguous term

Our use of the word 'sinner' tends to be ambiguous. Perhaps it might help to make a distinction between the positive and negative ways Christians use the word.

For Christians 'sin' is fundamentally a positive word. Its Christian meaning is inextricably bound up with our belief in a God of healing and forgiveness. Hence, the very 'owning' of one's sinfulness (and sin) before God is a transformative act. It is the first step on the road to conversion. To acknowledge that I am a sinner and to 'own' my sin before God is to confess my need for forgiveness and healing. The Gospel parable assures us that the person who, with the tax-collector, sincerely prays: 'Lord, be merciful to me a sinner' returns home 'at rights with God'.[2]

'Sinner' used in this positive way should not be taken to mean 'someone who used to be a sinner but is so no longer'. That is not what the tax-collector means when he prays, 'Lord, be merciful to me, a sinner.' He really is a sinner and he recognises himself as such. That is precisely why he recognises his need for the compassion and forgiveness of God. Even the words of Jesus to the woman taken in adultery, 'Go, and sin no more', are not an indication that she is no longer a sinner. She leaves Jesus a sinner, but a forgiven sinner, as do the many others who hear his life-giving words 'Go, your sins are forgiven you.'[3]

However, the word 'sinner' can be used by Christians also in a negative way. A striking example of a sinner in this negative sense is the Pharisee in the parable who prided himself on his righteous life and who thanked God that he was not like the rest of humankind. The Gospel tells us that he did not return home at rights with God. There is no indication in the parable that there is any major ethical misconduct in his life. His sin is at a deeper level than ethical misconduct. He personifies the people to whom Jesus is addressing this parable – 'people who prided themselves on being virtuous and despised everyone else.' It is this group of people who come under the negative use of the word 'sinner'. It is as though the only sin that ties the hands of God's forgiveness is the sin of grounding one's self-worth on a belief in the non-worth of everyone else.

Sinners in the positive sense mentioned earlier clearly belong to the Church. No one would have any problem with that. What about Christians who are sinners in the negative sense outlined above? Do they belong to the Church?

Fidelity to the gospel must surely make us recognise that they do. Yet at the same time, what are we to make of the fact that the Gospels portray Jesus as being radically opposed to this group of sinners? Perhaps it highlights the paradox in their situation. They belong to the Church and yet they are a living contradiction to the faith of the Church. Maybe the pastoral approach to these sinners has to reflect this paradox. At one and the same time, the Church has to both 'own' and 'disown' them and their sinfulness.

This is consistent with the process of conversion in the case of 'sinners' in the positive Christian sense. Sinners in that sense, when they 'own' their sinfulness and their sins, are both 'owning' and 'disowning' them at the same time. They are acknowledging that these sins truly are theirs. In owning their sins, they are recognising that these sins belong to them, they are part of their reality. Yet they are also acknowledging that, as disciples of Christ, they must also 'disown' these sins since they contradict what Christ stands for. That is why they want to 'die' to sin and be liberated from this side of their lives. Admittedly, the healing process might take a lifetime – and beyond! Yet the initial act of both 'owning' and 'disowning' their sin is indispensable. Without that first step the healing process cannot begin.

This conversion process is short-circuited in the case of 'sinners' in the negative sense. As long as they remain enclosed within their self-inflicted blindness, there is no possibility that they will 'disown' their sin since they refuse even to 'own' it. This is where the Church has to step in. As well as 'owning' their sin, the Church must also 'disown' it, precisely because it is also the Church's sin. In the case of conduct which, though wrong, does not involve any major violation of the dignity of human persons, it is probably sufficient for such 'disowning' to be implicit in the ordinary run-of-the-mill moral teaching of the Church as commonly recognised by people. However, where grosser violations of human dignity are involved, the Church might feel obliged to 'own' the sin by a very explicit act of 'naming' it (and even the sinner, in some instances) and at the same time 'disowning' it by declaring it to be contradictory to Christian life and witness.

A very striking instance of such 'owning' and 'disowning' by the Church is found in a sermon preached in 1511 on the island of Hispaniola (the modern-day Dominican Republic). The preacher, Fray Antonio de Montesinos, a Dominican friar, was addressing a congregation made up of the Governor of the island and all the Christian notables who were making themselves rich by their exploitation of the native Indians. Taking as his text 'I am the voice of one crying in the desert', he began:

> I am the voice of Christ crying in the desert of this island. It is essential that you listen . . .with your entire heart and your entire being . . .The message of Christ to you is this: you are all in a state of mortal sin. You are living in mortal sin and will die in it, because of your cruelty and your tyrannical attitude towards innocent people . . . Are they, too, not human beings? . . . Are you not obliged to love them as yourselves?[4]

It would be hard to imagine a more forthright condemnation of a group of people. The language is blunt, the judgement is clear and unconditional. Nevertheless, when this sermon is read in our own day when there is more readiness to acknowledge the collusion and even support of the Church for the appalling injustice committed against the Indians, it stands out like a beacon in the darkness. Fray Antonio had the integrity and courage to name the horrendous sin which was being committed against the Indians. And the context of his naming was the gathering of the community to celebrate the Eucharist. The Governor and the Christian nobility of the island had gathered to thank God for all the blessings they had received. I suspect that there would have been no Indians present at that gathering. The Christian invaders would have considered them 'not our kind'. No doubt, too, they would have thought of them as 'not God's kind' either, since they were sunk in idolatry and outside the grace of God. These Christian nobles, like the

Pharisee in the parable, would have thanked God that they were not 'like the rest of mankind' and particularly that they were not like these Indians.

To gather in Eucharist in such a frame of mind is a horrendous sacrilege. Such people, in the words of the parable, would not go home again 'at rights with God'. Fray Antonio says the same thing in different language when he tells them they will go home 'in a state of mortal sin'.

What so outraged Fray Antonio was that this eucharistic gathering of Christians refused to own their blatantly obvious sin. As long as they refused to take that step, they were not en route for conversion. They were facing in the opposite direction. They were in a state of mortal sin. No doubt, the pastoral intention behind his sermon was salvific. By naming their sin with such candour (and he was 'one of them'), he was hoping that they might be stirred into recognising the inhumanity they were involved in. His naming their sin was an invitation to them to own it themselves.

It could probably be argued that some papal encyclicals, particularly in the social field, fit into this process of 'owning' and 'disowning' gross sins of violating the dignity of human persons. So too do prophetic statements of local hierarchies and Church groups when they speak out against violations of human dignity in their own countries. Such 'owning' and 'disowning' is clearly seen as an integral element in proclaiming the gospel of God's love for all women and men. This is part of the Church's public witness. Of course, whether it has any credibility will largely depend on how faithful the Church is to the gospel it is proclaiming. Paul VI made this point very clearly in his Apostolic Letter on Evangelisation: 'People today listen more willingly to witnesses than to teachers, and if they do listen to teachers, it is because they are witnesses' (n. 41). This salutary warning leads us to look at the credibility of the Church's own life and conduct. Granted that it is a Church of sinners, does the 'owning' and 'disowning' of sin by the Church in its own life and conduct give a credible witness to those outside the Church to whom it is proclaiming the gospel?

Difficulties with the credibility of the Church's public witness

In the eyes of many outside the Church, including those sympathetically disposed towards it, there is a major problem about the credibility of the Church's public witness. This is due to the fact that the current categorisation of certain groups of people in the Church as 'sinners' seems to run counter to our present-day perception of what constitutes inhumanity. Many who come into these categories are not perceived by people today as involved in any gross violation of the dignity of the human person. In fact, in many instances they are seen more as 'victims of sin' and it is their own dignity as human persons which has been violated.

Among such people are women and men who have had to face the shattering experience of recognising that the marriage on which they have staked their lives has failed and whose painful pilgrimage through a kind of death towards resurrection has eventually led them into a second marriage; or, again, gay men and lesbian women who have struggled with their sexual identity in the face of incomprehension, disapproval and even outright hostility from many in society (perhaps their own family in some cases), who, in their loneliness and hopelessness, may have sought some kind of passing relief in a series of transient relationships and who have eventually found peace, a positive direction in life and genuine love in a more permanent gay or lesbian relationship which, in turn, is sustained and deepened by the sexual expression of their love; or married couples who have found that methods of contraception condemned by the Church have helped them deepen their love for each other and their children by giving them the opportunity to make love when appropriate without the experience being vitiated by the fear of another pregnancy. In their different ways, all these people have been made to feel that they are not fully accepted in the Church they regard as their home. They even experience this condemnation as a form of being 'disowned' by the Church.

For instance, those who are living in a second marriage,

unless they are widowed or their first marriage has been annulled, are officially barred from receiving communion. Gay couples in faithful relationships are 'disowned' by official Church teaching in very strong terms. In fact, the recent letter of the Congregation of the Doctrine of the Faith to the U.S. bishops even justifies discrimination against them in the area of housing and certain forms of employment. The implication clearly is that they constitute a danger to society and are likely to corrupt the morals of the young. Those who cannot accept the teaching of *Humanae Vitae* and who find the practice of contraception beneficial to their marriage are told by the Pope: 'What is called into question by the rejection of this teaching is the very idea of the holiness of God.'[5]

Of course, the point will be made that there is no problem for any of these people provided they are prepared to both 'own' and 'disown' their sin. If those in a second marriage are prepared to live as 'brother and sister', they can receive communion. If gays and lesbians renounce their lifestyle and practise celibacy, they will be fully accepted. If couples practising contraception would only take advantage of the enormous advances in the reliability and availability of natural family planning, the Church would have no moral objection to their deliberately avoiding having any further children.

However, the problem is not as simple as this solution seems to suggest. For the most part, these people have really tried to 'own' and 'disown' whatever sin may perhaps have been involved in the tragic situations they have lived through. In no way are they denying that they are sinners. Many of them feel their sinfulness very profoundly – but in the positive sense mentioned earlier. They can identify very deeply with the prayer of the tax-collector 'Lord, be merciful to me, a sinner'.

However what they cannot 'disown' is the gift of new life they are now experiencing. It runs counter to their own experience for such couples in a good second marriage or in a life-giving homosexual partnership to be told that they are 'living in sin', or for married couples to be told that their contraceptive-aided love-making is seriously offensive to God. Such people cannot 'disown' as sinful something which they actually experience and 'own' as grace-filled. Far from 'living in sin', they believe they are forgiven sinners living in grace. And they are grateful to God for this gift.

It is sometimes argued that the conduct of these categories of people has to be publicly 'disowned' because it is a living contradiction to the Church's moral witness. In reality, what scandalises many people outside the Church, as well as within, is the fact that a Church of sinners which professes belief in a God of forgiveness and compassion seems to condemn groups of people for whom most in our society would feel great compassion.

The sinfulness of office-holders in the Church

As Christians our love for the Church inclines us to presume the integrity of office-holders in the Church, especially since, from the nature of the case, they are usually bishops and priests. Hence, while theoretically we recognise the possibility of their sinning, our natural tendency is to deny, or at least play down, sin on the part of office-holders. I am not referring to sin in their personal lives but in the exercise of their duties of office.

There is no lack of criticism of office-holders in the Church. Like all who carry the heavy burden of exercising authority, they are targets for criticism from all quarters. However, we do not tend to speak of 'sin' with regard to the way they exercise their office. Perhaps this reticence betrays a kind of spiritual immaturity. We find our security in the Church. Hence, we do not like to think of those in positions of authority as capable of letting us down by actually sinning in the decisions they make.

Sinful behaviour means acting in a way which violates human dignity, either that of ourselves or of others. Quite literally it is irresponsible behaviour since it is failing to respond adequately to the needs of the human persons with whom we are dealing.

Hence, all sin is inhumanity in some form or other. In the past decade there have been an increasing number of allegations of serious inhumanity in the way office-holders at various levels in the Church have exercised their authority. The criteria used for the appointment of bishops and the actual appointments made in a not inconsiderable number of cases have been regarded as irresponsible and hence inhuman. The same has been alleged with regard to the way some female religious congregations have been treated as they have struggled to reorder their constitutions in response to their original charism and the needs of the present day. Something similar is alleged to have happened to some male congregations wanting to return to the 'non-clerical' vision of their founder. Numerous theologians of acknowledged competence and integrity appear to have been hounded in a most inhuman fashion by a CDF which fails to listen to the breadth of theological thinking in the Church as a whole. If these allegations are true, and I am inclined to think they are, the situation is serious.

However, the core of the inhumanity alleged to be currently operative among some office-holders in the Church, especially in some of the Vatican congregations, lies deeper than these particular instances. They are the symptoms, rather than the root cause.

The root cause is perceived by many people as being a mind-set found among many powerful Vatican office-holders which is not open to views which challenge its own position. Any listening that takes place is not for the purpose of learning but only in order to refute. Local churches struggling to bring about more genuine inculturation of the gospel or who are trying to interpret the gospel in the light of the signs of the times as experienced in their part of the world, find their efforts emasculated by curial directives or by manipulation on the part of some curial congregations or officials. According to first-hand reports, the curial manipulation of the 1992 meeting of the Latin American Episcopal Council (CELAM) seems to have been a blatant example of such an irresponsible and inhuman exercise of authority. Issues which, in the Church at large throughout the world, are considered to be burning issues of pastoral urgency are not even allowed on the agenda for discussion – optional celibacy for priests, the ordination of women, not forgetting the issues mentioned in the previous section, contraception, remarriage after divorce and homosexuality.

This kind of inhumanity on the part of some office-holders is beginning to drive many in the Church to desperation. It even provoked such a saintly moral theologian as the late Bernard Häring to overcome his natural reluctance to criticise the Vatican publicly. His little book, *My Witness for the Church*, was extremely frank and hard-hitting in its criticisms of the mentality of some office-holders in the Vatican.[6] He felt an obligation to 'do all that is humanly possible to encourage a change, a transformation of the structures and mentalities which are not gospel-centred' and even went so far as to say: 'I believe that we have arrived at the point where it can no longer be disputed that we are in a pathological situation.'[7]

To believe in a Church of sinners is to recognise that there is a real possibility of sin in the office-holders of the Church. Consequently, a concern for the good of the Church should make us alert to situations where this possibility may seem to be actually realised. This should not be condemned out of hand as a negative, hypercritical or disloyal attitude towards the Church. Of course, it is possible that some people who criticise office-holders in the Church may in reality be dumping on them unresolved problems from their earlier years. However, that is merely a pathological version of what is fundamentally a very positive and healthy love of a Church which is honestly acknowledged to be a Church of sinners. I interpret Bernard Häring's impassioned criticisms as an expression of such a love of the Church.

Granting the real possibility of sin in the office-holders of the Church, such sin, when it occurs, contradicts the public witness of the Church and so needs to be publicly 'owned' and 'disowned'. If this is done by the office-holders themselves, there is no problem. In fact, in 1996 and 1997 the Church saw a breakthrough in this regard. The bishops of England and Wales issued a public apology to divorced Catholics for any hurt they had suffered as a result of pastoral insensitivity on the part of the Catholic community;[8] a group of French bishops owned the shame of the failure of their local churches during the time of the Nazi occupation;[9] on 1 November 1997 Pope John Paul II apologised for Christian anti-Jewish prejudice;[10] and similar sentiments were expressed, with specific reference to the

Holocaust, by the new Papal Nuncio to Britain, Archbishop Pablo Puente, in one of his first public addresses to a mainly Jewish audience: 'At the beginning of the third millennium, the Catholic Church is committed to an important examination of conscience, of clarification and of profound self-criticism regarding the past.'[11] When, on the contrary, Church authorities refuse to 'own' their sin and even insist on denying it, it needs to be named and 'owned' by other members of the Church, so that it can then be publicly 'disowned' for the sake of the public witness of the Church. However, a catch-22 situation arises when the office-holders concerned claim to be judge and jury in their own case. This is really what happens when they claim the right to set the agenda regarding what issues are open for discussion in the Church. The catch-22 situation is intensified when they attempt to make lesser office-holders promise under oath to keep to the restricted agenda they have set. The ultimate irony occurs when they publicly 'disown' the very people who have the prophetic insight and courage to 'own' and 'disown' the Church-injuring sins of these office-holders.

Is 'sin' too harsh a word to be using in this context? I do not think so. My intention is not to vilify these office-holders or attribute personal malice to them. Sin is a word with all kinds of positive reverberations for Christians. To speak of sin with regard to office-holders in the Church is to acknowledge their solidarity with the rest of us. Unlike what we say of Christ in the Fourth Eucharistic Prayer, they are like us in all things, including sin. To make sin a taboo word in speaking of them is to refuse to face human reality. It also shows a lack of faith in the power of God's healing Spirit active in the Church – and a lack of faith in the office-holders in question to be open to that Spirit.

The Church we believe in – a Church of sinners, but also a holy Church

Although most of this chapter has been looking at the sinfulness of the Church, I would like to end on a much more positive note.

The ultimate object of faith is God. God is the one in whom we believe. To believe in the Church is to believe in God acting in and through the Church. To borrow a phrase from Rahner, the Holy Spirit is the dynamic element in the Church. That is why it is totally inadequate to counter criticisms about the sinfulness of the Church by saying that, on balance, there is more good than evil within it. Our belief in the holiness of the Church is not a judgement of proportionality. It is belief in the living presence and action of God in the Church. That is why any pessimism or fatalism with regard to the Church must be 'disowned' as unchristian. It stands in contradiction to belief in the Church. While we must 'own' its sinfulness – and each of us has a special responsibility to 'own' his or her personal contribution to that sinfulness – we must not be content to settle for that sinfulness and give it whatever house-room it wants in the Church. Our belief in the Holy Spirit, present and active in the Church, commits us strongly to 'disown' that sinfulness. To believe in the Church is to have a confident hope that the Church can become a truer image of the one whose very name it 'owns' by calling itself Christian. Hence, we must always have the faith and courage to 'disown' whatever is unchristian in the Church. This must be the case even, or rather especially, when what is deemed to be unchristian is the way office-holders in the Church are exercising their authority. The words of Cardinal Ratzinger, quoted by Leonardo Boff in a letter to his Franciscan Provincial, might provide an appropriate conclusion to this chapter:

> Is it unconditionally a sign of better times that today's theologians no longer dare to speak prophetically? Is it not rather a sign of a feeble love which no longer makes the heart burn with holy zeal for God's cause (2 Cor. 12:2)? It is the sign of a love which has become apathetic and which no longer dares to make the painful commitment on behalf of and in favour of the beloved. The person who does not feel wounded by the shortcomings of a friend, who no longer suffers because of them and who does not fight to change them, no longer loves. Should this also apply to our relationship with the Church?[12]

PART 3

Moral Theology at the Service of Pastoral Ministry

7

Moral Theology and Pastoral Care in the Parish

My experience of combining pastoral work as a diocesan priest in an inner-city parish with teaching students at undergraduate and postgraduate level has convinced me that the role of moral theology will vary according to the context in which it is operating.

For many centuries moral theology was bound up with the training of confessors. It was designed to aid confessors in their task of helping penitents confess their sins according to the requirements of integrity. Although it was bound up with a tribunal model of the sacrament, it still had plenty of compassion and pastoral sensitivity built into it. Most moral theology manuals contained comments in small print, usually accommodating seemingly hard-line principles to the demands of pastoral flexibility. Clearly, in this context the role of moral theology was to instruct the priest as confessor.

With the post-Vatican II 'reconciliation' model of the sacrament and with more attention being given to healing and the social dimension of sin, the needs of the confessor changed to a large extent. This, in turn, had its impact on moral theology. Nevertheless, its basic context remained the same: it was still serving priests in their pastoral ministry.

There had always been a number of particular contexts in

This essay first appeared in the October 1994 special issue of *Priests and People* (pp. 367–72) dealing with moral theology. Its original title was 'Moral Theology in the Parish'. I have added a few paragraphs which, due to lack of space, were omitted from the original.

which moral theology was also seen to have a role. For instance, in the field of medical ethics, especially with regard to issues affecting the beginning or end of life or reproductive medicine, moral theologians were asked to provide the Church's teaching on various controversial issues. The context here was a model of a teaching Church which felt able to provide authoritative teaching on all kinds of ethical questions in this field. This context, too, has changed in recent years. While the importance of medical ethics has increased rather than diminished, there has been a growing recognition that the Church's role in this field is to make its own specific contribution to a common search for truth and rightness in these perplexing problems. Hence, it needs to be also a learning Church if it is to exercise this role competently. In this new context, moral theology cannot operate as a self-sufficient discipline. It needs to be involved at an interdisciplinary level and also in dialogue with other Christians, other faiths and all people of good will.

Everyday lives

However, the context I would like to concentrate on in this chapter is that of ordinary Catholic men and women in their everyday lives. Most of these people are unlikely ever to read a volume on moral theology. That does not imply that moral theology has no place in their lives. The consistent message coming through both Old and New Testament writers is that we profess our belief in God by the way we live our lives. Part of the role of moral theology is to help people discern how this is best done in the nitty-gritty of everyday life.

Moral theology, therefore, is very much involved with the context of people's ordinary lives. However, the key question is: how does it operate in this context? In a purely hierarchical model of the Church, it will be presumed that moral theology enters this context through 'teaching moments'. It is conveyed to people through religious instruction, homilies, adult Christian education sessions and so forth. However, this is still defining the role of moral theology from the point of view of ministry. It sees providing sound moral teaching as part of the

Church's pastoral ministry to ordinary people. According to this model, therefore, the main impetus for moral theology in the Church still comes from the 'teaching' elite, whether they are seen to be those with official teaching authority or those who are professional moral theologians.

While I would not want to disparage any of that or suggest that there is not an appropriate and important place for it, nevertheless I believe the picture of moral theology it presents is incomplete. It does not do justice to the place of moral theology in the lives of ordinary men and women.

Examples

A simple down-to-earth example from real life might help to highlight the unease I feel about a too reductionist view of moral theology in people's lives.

John and Mary come to me and say they want to be married. They have been living together for the past eight years and have a lovely daughter who is doing very well at our local Catholic school. They are about to move into their new home, the first time they will have a decent house to live in. Mary assumes that they cannot have a Nuptial Mass and that she will not be able to wear white for the wedding. Every pastorally sensitive priest will want to be open and welcoming to John and Mary. However, the critical question is: what about the eight years they have been living together? Clearly, Mary is presuming that the Church will condemn their life together during those years. They have been 'living in sin'. However, that externally imposed label might not correspond to what has been taking place in the core of their lives together before God. Maybe moral theology has an interpretative role to play here, trying to understand what has really been going on in their lives. Perhaps a truer interpretation of what has been happening at the most fundamental level could be that, despite the ambiguity of their situation, they have been growing together in mutual love. If that were the case, the most important thing going on when they get married will not be 'putting right' what was wrong. Rather, as well as taking the important step of formally and publicly expressing their mutual commitment in love for the future, they will want to be thanking God for and celebrating so much giftedness in their previous eight years together, including the precious gift of their daughter. And, if this is so, their daughter should obviously have an important role in the marriage ceremony itself. They would also probably want to ask God's forgiveness and healing for the shadow side of their life together during the past eight years. That is not surprising. After all, there would be much that needs forgiveness and healing in the life of any married couple who have been together for eight years.

This might seem an isolated case but that is far from true. For a variety of reasons, cohabitation is an increasingly common phenomenon these days, even among Catholics. A glance at most baptismal registers in my area of Liverpool would give ample proof of that. For me the key question is: can moral theology be content to stand outside this situation and pass judgement on it? Or is an important part of moral theology to be concerned about what is actually taking place within the ambiguity of the lives of cohabiting couples like John and Mary? And does part of the role of the professional moral theologian (and the Church) also involve listening and trying to understand and appreciate whatever is good in what is happening?

In the parable of the wheat growing among the darnel,[1] the owner's servants saw a field overgrown with darnel and wanted to pull it all out, overlooking the harm this would do to the wheat. The owner, on the other hand, – and he is the one whose attitude reflects the kingdom of heaven – sees a field full of wheat, thriving against a backcloth of darnel. 'Encourage the wheat to grow,' he says, 'we can get rid of the darnel when the wheat has fully ripened.' There might well be a fair measure of darnel in John and Mary's relationship, as in all our lives. However, in this context, part of the pastoral role of moral theology would seem to be to value and care for the wheat and help it to grow.

Let me offer another example, again from the context of human relationships. A few years ago I received a letter asking my advice about the following problem. (To respect confidentiality I have altered many details but it remains substantially the situation that was put to me.)

John, a eucharistic minister, is a widower with a teenage son, Paul, living at home with him. Paul was deeply upset by his mother's death and was quite a problem for a while. However, now he has settled down. He and his father have a good relationship and they share their home very peacefully. Paul obviously feels their home belongs to him as much as to his father and this gives him a sense of security. John has developed a close friendship with Maureen, another eucharistic minister, herself a widow. Their friendship has grown into a deep love. This is creating a dilemma for them. From time to time they make love together which, as Maureen says, 'is entirely natural and loving but against the rules of the Church.' Whenever this happens, they both go to confession as soon as possible and receive absolution. The response from priests in the confessional has varied from 'hell and damnation to much milder rebukes'. As Maureen puts it, 'As two people struggling to be good Catholics, we worry about this situation and do not want to imperil our eternal salvation.' Neither think marriage would be advisable, certainly for the present. John is worried that it might cause problems for Paul again; and Maureen is put off by the experience of a close friend where a similar marriage proved disastrous. Because they are deeply committed to each other and past the age of childbearing, they wonder whether there might be more flexibility about the way they express their love for each other.

In line with the pastoral role of moral theology I have been suggesting above, part of my reply was as follows:

> You ask me to react to what you have called your 'dilemma'. I am sure you know me well enough not to expect me to give you an 'outside ruling', as it were. That would not be doing justice to you both and your own responsibility and privilege to make your own responsible decisions with as much honesty and integrity as you can – and then 'own' those decisions before God. If I were to pass judgement, I would simply be encouraging

you both to regress to a level of moral immaturity.

I am sure you must both feel in your heart of hearts that it does not really make much sense for the two of you to make love together, recognising that this is, as you say, 'entirely natural and loving' and then to rush to confession as soon as possible afterwards. Somehow that is allowing yourselves to live with two different (contradictory?) visions of God at the same time. You are obviously both persons who are deeply committed to living lives which are pleasing to God.

Your problem seems to be that you are experiencing your making love as something good and wholesome which brings healing and positive value to both your lives. Your inner understanding of God seems to be telling you that this is good and cannot be displeasing to God, since God, according to this vision, is a God of healing, love and positive life. But you are also faced with what you call 'the rules of the Church' which seem to be saying that what you are doing is sinful and so displeasing to God. So at one level you are thankful to God for this experience of loving and being loved; and at another level you feel guilty before God.

It seems to me that you have to make up your minds which of these two visions of God is the one you really believe in. Aquinas once wrote: 'God is not offended by us except insofar as we harm ourselves or each other.'[2] It would seem to me that if you really believe in the vision of God which fits in with what Aquinas says (and I suspect you do), the consequence is not simply to say, 'Fine. There is no problem about our making love in the way we are doing.' I would think you would both need to be asking yourselves some searching questions about what you are doing – and answering those questions as honestly and openly as you can to each other.

You probably know that the main reason Jack Dominian would offer for saying that making love outside of marriage is not good (that is, wholesome and upbuilding) is because making love is a way of saying something very deep to each other through the intimate language of sexual loving. And, so his argument goes, what is said through making love is

> something about total giving and total receiving and total sharing through the shared joy and vulnerability of sexual loving. You might decide that since you have both been previously married (and, presumably, having been blessed with good marriages) and since as a couple you are beyond the age of starting a family, the meaning of making love in your case is somewhat altered. This might make you decide that the objection that making love outside marriage is saying something untrue does not really apply to your case. You may feel that what you are saying to each other is very true and it is the most you are capable of saying to each other in your particular situations.
>
> I suppose what I am saying is that, according to this vision of God and God's will, you have to think carefully to make sure that, in the long run, you will not both be doing something hurtful to each other by promising something through making love which either one or both of you is not able or prepared to give but which your making love leads one or both of you to expect in some way or other.

I could offer a variety of other examples. For instance, in an article entitled 'Looking beyond Failure', I tried to wrestle with the problem of marriage breakdown, including situations in which a second marriage seems to be the only life-giving way forward.[3] I ended that article by saying that the death-resurrection message of the Church is not a consolidation of the experience of failure. Rather it offers a positive interpretation of that negative experience. It could perhaps be paraphrased somewhat along the following lines:

> You are shattered by your failure. You may feel worthless. This painful experience might lead you to believe that you are not capable of taking on a commitment to life-long fidelity and sustaining it. Do not believe all that about yourself. The Lord invites you to believe in him and to believe in yourself. You are not alone. He is with you to strengthen you as you continue your journey through life. Arise! Come forth and live. Leave behind your old self, that half-truth you were living. You have lost that false self and found your true self.

> Live your new and true life by loving 'as I have loved you'. Have confidence to follow that love wherever it leads you. If your new life turns out to be a life lived in the single state, whether alone or as parent to your children, live it out with complete belief in your own dignity and that of those around you. Live out your singleness as the gift of the richness of yourself to the present and the future. Refuse to let all the love you can share as a single person be devalued by 'negative' utopian thinking. That would turn it into a life-denying noose placed round your neck by the restraining obligation of a partnership which no longer exists.
>
> If your new life eventually leads you to a new life-giving relationship, accept that with gratitude and live it out in faith – faith in yourself, in your partner and in your God who is entrusting this gift of love to you in the new chapter of your life which you are co-authoring together.

Pastoral theology?

It might be objected that what I am talking about here is pastoral theology, not moral theology. The problem with dismissing the above approach as pastoral theology lies in its implication that moral theology is not pastoral! Although normative ethics has an important place in moral theology, it is not the whole of it.

Normative ethics attempts to state what kinds of behaviour are conducive or harmful to human flourishing. Those which are conducive are said to be ethically right; those which are harmful are ethically wrong. Obviously, such statements are necessarily universal. They apply across the board. However, they are not necessarily absolute. This is because the description of behaviour contained in such statements, though accurate in so far as it goes, may not always go far enough. There might be aspects of the behaviour in question which are not contained in this description and these aspects might be ethically very significant. Mutilation is often cited as an example. In itself, mutilation is harmful to human wellbeing. However, a mutilation which can be more adequately described as a life-saving amputation is obviously beneficial rather than harmful.

Furthermore, precisely because normative ethics is necessarily limited to the sphere of universals, it cannot be expected to take adequate account of the particularities of individual personal existence. It can say that, all things being equal, certain forms of behaviour can rightly and universally be described as beneficial or harmful to human wellbeing. But at the level of individual human persons all things are not always equal. And in some instances this inequality may have a major bearing on ethical analysis.

For instance, all things being equal, the demands of the Christian love ethic are made more specific by normative ethics in terms of loving behaviour as is appropriate for a heterosexual person, whether he or she is married, single or committed to consecrated celibacy. However, all things are not equal for a person who, for whatever reason, finds him or herself constitutionally homosexual. If it is true that this state is irreversible and affects one's personal identity at a very profound level, then it would seem to follow that for such a person the demands of the Christian love ethic will be made specific in terms of loving behaviour which is appropriate for a homosexual person. Moreover, it might even be argued that, if it is also true that, for a fully committed homosexual couple, sexually expressed love can be genuinely self-giving, non-exploitative, faithful and promoting real personal growth, then it would seem to follow that true Christian love could be expressed by such behaviour. For many such a statement might seem shocking and contrary to the Church's tradition. However, it is important to remember that for most of its history the Christian Church would have been similarly shocked by any suggestion that the true Christian love which binds a married couple together could be expressed through sexual intercourse. The traditional Christian position was that the only justification for tolerating such behaviour which debased the mind by its animal intensity was for the sake of having children or to stop one's partner from straying into another's bed!

Exceptions

Normative ethics is capable of dealing with apparent exceptions to its universal norms. These exceptions are themselves a form of universal modification to a universal rule. However, the question arises: how do these exceptions make themselves known? Does some creative thinker sit down and work out some logically consistent, carefully formulated exception to a universal rule? Or does the undeniable goodness in a particular instance make its presence known and this goodness demand to be recognised – and not just in this unique instance but in every instance where the morally relevant special features are found to be verified. I think Jack Mahoney identifies this process very precisely when he writes:

> . . . moral principles are made for situations, and not situations for moral principles . . . Moreover, really new situations challenge established moral principles to give an account of themselves . . . in terms of the underlying reasoning which gives rise to such principles. In other words, . . . there is a continual dialectical process between principles and situations, between facts and moral reflection, a two-way traffic rather than simply a one-way application of principles. In identifying a discrepancy between the situation as it really is and the situation as it is described (and *ipso facto* evaluated), not only is it established that this situation does not 'come under' the moral principle in mind, but the moral principle itself is subjected to scrutiny and refinement . . . In one sense all this can be summed up in the old adage that 'circumstances alter cases', but there is more to it than that . . . circumstances also alter principles.[4]

It is an abuse of the term 'pastoral theology' to envisage it as a pastoral approach which is quite separate from moral theology and which implicitly outlaws moral theology from the pastoral context by allowing unjustified exceptions to the general rules so painstakingly arrived at. Moral theology must not allow itself to be banished from the pastoral context in this way. One part of the pastoral role of moral theology is to engage in the difficult process of discernment by which what might at first seem to be violations of universal principles are recognised to be a 'rule unto themselves'. That does not mean that they escape from the realm of universality. Rather, their undeniable truth establishes their universal authority in their own right. Consequently, there needs to be a corresponding realignment of existing general norms to make allowance for the universal authority of this aspect of moral truth. This does not mean that every universal norm has to be denuded of its important social impact by dying the death of a thousand qualifications. Aristotle and Aquinas were aware of that danger. That is why they did not try to codify all these apparent exceptions but left them to the aspect of the virtue of justice which they called 'epikeia'. Today a more appropriate term for that might perhaps be 'pastoral sensitivity'. It strikes me that the small print sections of the moral theology manuals served as a useful aid in developing this pastoral sensitivity. Perhaps we contemporary moral theologians have not served the Church in the way we should by offering pastorally relevant examples of such apparent exceptions. I believe many people have, in fact, learned this virtue of pastoral discernment in their own lives but moral theologians might have offered them more help in this process.

Healthy growth

However, even this does not fully capture what I want to say about part of the pastoral role of moral theology. Perhaps it might help to go back to the parable of the wheat and the darnel. Normative ethics helps us recognise both wheat and darnel. However, the owner of the field is doing something other than recognising their joint presence in his field. The focus of his concern is elsewhere. He has faith in the healthy growth of his wheat, despite all the darnel mixed in with it. His principal concern is to protect his wheat from the misguided zeal of those intent on destroying the darnel without any regard for the harm this might do to the wheat.

Normative ethics is moral theology in its role of distinguishing right from wrong, allowing for all the complexities of moral analysis touched on above. However, moral theology also has a gospel-inspired role of believing in human goodness and of safeguarding the slow growth of this goodness in the midst of all the ambiguities of human life. This is an important aspect of the pastoral role of moral theology. To overlook this is to opt for a reductionist view of moral theology and to restrict it totally to the realm of normative ethics. I would dare to suggest that at least some of our pastoral problems at parish level come from over-zealous promoters of such a reductionist vision of moral theology. They misinterpret its pastoral role as being one of uprooting the evil identified by normative ethics, regardless of the fact that the good is embedded in the same soil and is in danger of being uprooted by what they are doing.

One of the privileges I value most as a priest is that of being invited by a family to preside at the funeral of one of their members who has died. This truly is a privilege since I am being asked to lead them in the celebration of the unique goodness of this person's life, despite all the ambiguity and shadow-side which have also been there. Such a celebration is not dishonestly portraying as a saint a person everyone knew was a sinner. It is more a matter of seeing through the sinful side of a person (which is so obvious, to a greater or lesser extent, in all of us) and discerning the genuine goodness which lies beneath the surface. There may be much more darnel in some people's lives than in others. But there may also be far more wheat in the middle of such an abundance of darnel than in some cases where the growth of both darnel and wheat has been pretty sparse. (Most priests have come across cases of the 'I never do anyone any harm' syndrome!)

I believe this experience has affected very profoundly my understanding of moral theology in the parish context, especially in the kinds of parishes where I have served and in which life has been an uphill struggle for most people. If moral theology is called to discern and celebrate the underlying goodness found in the life of a person who has died, despite all the ambiguity that may be there, surely it is also called to discern and celebrate that same goodness during a person's lifetime. To believe in that goodness and to encourage its growth would seem to be a crucial pastoral role for moral theology.

Messy and dirty

One pastoral role of normative ethics is to help us be aware of the darnel and not mistake it for wheat. While heeding the gospel warning that it can be harmful to the wheat if we try to eradicate the darnel, at least we recognise darnel when we see it. This can then help us to identify where the darnel is coming from and what are the underlying causes responsible for its getting into this particular field. One way normative ethics operates pastorally is by providing an important diagnostic service for social analysis. This is a very important social function. Moreover, normative ethics can also be rather like the beautiful picture found on the outside of a seed packet. It can motivate us to plant the seed in the first place. But part of the pastoral role of moral theology is to help the seed to grow, despite soil deficiency, adverse weather, surrounding weeds and lots of other threatening dangers. It would be tragically ironic if moral theology itself became yet another danger by threatening to uproot the growing plant by turning over the soil and pulling up the weeds. Moral theology is not meant to condemn the plant emerging from the seed simply because it does not live up to the promise of the idealised picture on the packet. Rather it appreciates the growth that occurs. Sometimes what might look like a puny and undeveloped plant might, in fact, be a miracle of growth, given the adverse conditions under which it has had to struggle.

For the most part, the 'normative ethics' role of moral theology necessarily has to be very exact and precise. Clarity of analysis is very important. However, the role of promoting growth in adverse conditions can sometimes be a much more messy procedure. At times it can involve getting one's hands dirty, cutting corners, adopting a flexible approach to Church rules and so on. It also needs faith and a sense of humour in the face of accusations that one is compromising the truth, or falling into the error of relativism or situation ethics. Perhaps part of the role of a moral theologian in the parish context might even be to encourage people 'not to take the Church too seriously'! We take the Church too seriously when we turn it into an idol and give it the respect and reverence due to God alone.

I hope these reflections might be helpful in some pastoral contexts. They may be quite inappropriate in others. For instance, some sayings of Jesus seem to suggest that what might be called for in certain instances would be a more radical approach, more akin to invasive surgery (cf. Matt. 5:29-30). In some instances the growth of the seed might be being choked and destroyed by the entangling thorns (cf. Matt. 13:22). A good friend of mine often advises me: Never say 'never'! Perhaps one should never say 'always' either! In other words, although the pastoral approach outlined above may not always be appropriate, I firmly believe that sometimes it is not only appropriate but actually necessary for a person's spiritual wellbeing.

8

The Changing Face of Moral Theology

The title of one of Richard Niebuhr's sermons is 'The Shaking of the Foundations'. That could be an apt title for what has been happening in moral theology during the past forty years. I have had the good fortune to live through that 'moving' experience.

My initial studies in moral theology began in the seminary in 1954 and were most definitely pre-Vatican II. Although as students we could feel the ground beginning to move in our biblical studies, those initial tremors did not affect our course in moral theology. After ordination I was sent for postgraduate studies to Fribourg University in Switzerland. There my further studies in moral theology, though chronologically prior to Vatican II, helped to prepare me for the momentous upheaval which was soon to take place. My Dominican tutors in Fribourg helped me to take a closer look at the foundations of my theology, which, in turn, opened my eyes to an appreciation that these solid foundations, symbolised by Aquinas's magnificent synthesis in his *Summa Theologica*, could be properly understood only by seeing them within their historical context.

The first part of this chapter is an edited version of an article which first appeared in *Priests and People*, 1996, 318–23, under the title 'Being a Moral Theologian Today'. I have added sections (8) and (9) which contain revised material from my chapter 'The Role of the Moral Theologian in the Life of the Church' in Raphael Gallagher and Brendan McConvery (eds.), *History and Conscience: Studies in honour of Sean O'Riordan* CSSR (Dublin: Gill & Macmillan, 1989) and from my article 'Conformity and Dissent in the Church', in *The Way*, April 1988, 87–101.

Aquinas was a man of his time, wrestling with the problems of his day and drawing on the best of tradition and contemporary learning, secular as well as religious.

The moral theology I had been taught at the seminary was timeless. It contained the truth, the whole truth and nothing but the truth. All that needed to be done was to apply that truth to the particular problems of everyday life. Such a task required considerable subtlety since the truth in moral matters was articulated in the form of various basic principles, and it was sometimes difficult to see how these could all be respected in conflict situations. Grappling with such difficult cases was the art of the casuist. The older I get, the more I appreciate the vast learning and practical wisdom of the best practitioners of pre-Vatican II moral theology. Many of these moral theologians were men of great stature, who provided an invaluable service to the priests of their day. However, like Aquinas, they too were men of their time.

The times Aquinas lived through were times of theological ferment and intense debate. Although it would be an anachronism to ascribe 'historical consciousness' to Aquinas, it is certainly true that he was very much alive to the fact that he was living in a time of change. The questions being asked by theologians at that time were deep and probing. Aquinas never tried to outlaw any of these questions from the theological agenda. If they were questions of real significance, he tried to wrestle with them, believing that they were the pathway to a deeper understanding of the truth. Theology was very much 'faith seeking understanding'. Grasping what the real questions were was an important function of theology. It is no accident that Aquinas revelled in the scholastic methodology of 'quaestiones disputatae', that is, wrestling with burning contemporary questions. It is a great credit to his theological and philosophical acumen that many of the questions he grappled with remain on our agenda today and we are still able to draw great benefit from his insights on these issues.

My Fribourg immersion into the real contextual world of Aquinas (unlike the unreal timeless world of the late scholastics) helped to prepare me for the shaking of the foundations at

Vatican II. Some readers might not like the image of the shaking of the foundations, perhaps finding it too unsettling, even destructive. I warm to it. To me it suggests an upheaval which can itself be stabilising insofar as it shows up where the weaknesses lie and hence enables the foundations to settle once again in their new and consolidated realignment. It also reminds us that living with God's Spirit is like living on a seismic fault line. We can expect many more shakings of the foundations in the future.

The medieval saying, 'We see further than our forebears; we are like dwarfs sitting on the shoulders of giants' offers wise guidance for moral theologians following the shaking of the foundations at Vatican II. It reminds us that we are not wiser or more learned than our predecessors. When I look at the writings of my forebears in moral theology, I certainly feel like a dwarf in comparison with some of them. However, thanks to Vatican II and the age in which we are living, moral theologians today can see in a way which was humanly impossible in earlier ages. However, we will only be able to benefit from this new field of vision if we are true to where we are now in history. That means recognising that we are inheritors of the tradition that our predecessors have passed on to us but recognising, too, that this is a living tradition. God's Spirit is active within it and, in our own day, for Roman Catholics most notably in the Spirit-inspired event of Vatican II. Through the continuing inspiration of the Spirit, we are offered the gift of discernment enabling us to be appreciative of the strengths and richness of the tradition we have inherited while also being critically aware of its weaknesses.

This shaking of the foundations through Vatican II and its aftermath has obviously had a major impact on moral theology and the work of moral theologians. It is true that there is only one direct reference to moral theology in the documents of Vatican II. That is in the decree on *Priestly Formation* (*Optatam Totius*) which insists that 'special attention needs to be given to the development of moral theology', and goes on to say that 'its scientific exposition should be more thoroughly nourished by scriptural teaching' and that 'it should show the nobility of the Christian vocation of the faithful, and their obligation to bring forth fruit in charity for life of the world' (n. 16). Though these are very general statements, they communicate the message that the Council Fathers want moral theology to be nourished by the solid findings of modern scientific biblical scholarship. They want it also to be a positive encouragement, inspiration and challenge to the lives of lay-people living in the world. No longer should it be confined by the narrow, and narrowing, focus of training priests for their work as confessors, a focus which tended to concentrate too much on the sin-dimension of life.

I would like to look at how nine influential factors operative over recent years have radically renewed moral theology, radically changing it from how I and my contemporaries experienced it in the 1950s. I believe that the changes resulting from this radical renewal, as well as being faithful to the spirit of the living tradition we have inherited, have made moral theology more accessible and practically helpful to those working in pastoral ministry. Moral theology today is more in tune with the everyday concerns of people in general, both within and beyond the Church. Sadly, however, this renewal in moral theology has met some strong resistance within the Church and has not been fully embraced at all levels of Church life.

(1) Vatican II

Although moral theologians like myself recognise that moral theology has been challenged and enriched by the Second Vatican Council, we can still forget how fortunate we are. We constantly need to remind ourselves that we are living in a very privileged time in the history of moral theology. Many of the other headings elaborated below are linked in some way to Vatican II. However, to my mind, one point stands out above all others with regard to the impact of Vatican II on moral theology. That is its insistence that the primary criterion for moral evaluation is the good of the human person. Its focus, therefore, is on persons. This is not a rejection of objective morality. Far from it. It is opposed to the kind of subjective morality which would claim that the human subject alone can arbitrarily decide what constitutes moral rightness or moral goodness. For Vatican II morality is not subjective in the sense that, as subjects, we are free to create our own morality to suit our own convenience. Such an approach succumbs to a reductionist approach to the human person, seeing the person purely as subject, without any reference to all the other dimensions of human personhood, material, corporeal, relational, social, historico-cultural, unique and transcendental. Vatican II insists that morality must be objective in a way which views the human person holistically. In other words, the criterion of objective morality is the nature of the human person 'integrally and adequately considered'.[1]

This means that specific human actions, sexual intercourse, for example, are not to be evaluated by some kind of inbuilt moral criterion of their own which would operate in isolation from the good of the human person viewed more holistically. Because such a criterion is not looking to the good of the human person, integrally and adequately considered, it could lead to some unfortunate and even inhuman conclusions. [2]

Other ways in which Vatican II has challenged and enriched the work of moral theologians include:

- its teaching on the dignity of conscience and its freedom;
- the right and even responsibility of individual lay-people and priests to offer their own contribution to the Church's ongoing work of moral understanding and evaluation;
- its insistence that individuals have to shoulder responsibility for their own decisions and must not always expect detailed moral guidance from their bishops or priests;
- its recognition that the agenda for moral reflection and action comes mainly from the world (its joys and hopes, its sorrows and fears) rather than from the Church;
- its person-centred approach to marriage with its consequent emphasis on the paradigm of covenant/relationship rather than that of contract;
- its embracing of a Christian-humanist approach to life and its rejection of any approach based on a radical dichotomy between this life and the next;
- its rejection of an individualist approach to morality that

overlooks the social dimension of the human person and so is blind to the evil of structural sin.

(2) The experience and reflection of women

When I first began teaching moral theology, to my shame it never entered my head that women might have any contribution to make to the field of moral theology, let alone that they should actually become moral theologians. Thankfully, a rich collection of women friends, parishioners and colleagues have helped to change my thinking on this matter. Consequently, in *New Directions in Moral Theology*, Chapter 5 is entitled 'Moral theology – not truly human without the full participation of women'. At the beginning of that chapter I argue that Christian theology – and therefore moral theology too – is 'substantially flawed because it has been constructed predominately by men and in the light of men's experience of a world in which women were second-rate citizens and in which women's experience was not considered to be theologically important' (p. 86).

I believe that women's experience must be firmly in place on the agenda of moral theology. Moreover, it must not be there simply for male moral theologians to consider. Women must be fully represented within the field of moral theology – not just as a token gesture. That is beginning to happen. There are some outstanding women Roman Catholic moral theologians in the United States, for instance, Lisa Sowle Cahill and Margaret Farley. In the United Kingdom Linda Hogan, Julie Clague and Liz Stuart are making a name for themselves. If one extended the net to include women moral theologians from other Christian Churches, the picture would be even more encouraging.

When I referred earlier to the moral theologians of my seminary days as 'men of their time' I was not using exclusive language. I was simply describing the situation as it was. Moral theology was an all-male preserve.

In an earlier book, *Life and Love: Towards a Christian dialogue on bioethical questions*, dealing with in-vitro fertilisation, I included a chapter entitled 'What some women are saying about IVF'.[3] There I again registered my conviction that our ethical reflection is impoverished if the experience and voice of women is not heard. That is true right across the board, but it is particularly true in the field of reproductive technology:

> ...it is essential that women should play a full part in the debate about IVF. Until this happens in the Churches as well, what the Churches contribute to the debate will be neither fully Christian nor fully human. It will be only partial – and partiality impedes clear vision...I suppose this chapter contains a two-fold request. It is a request to women to continue to make their voice heard. And it is a request to the Churches (male-dominated as they all are, though in different ways and to different degrees) to make sure both that the voice of women is heard and that women's ears are fully represented on the official Church bodies which have the task of listening to what the Spirit is saying to the Churches through women. Until women are properly represented at that level, the official statements of the Churches will be defective in their understanding of human life and God's world and consequently the inspiration and guidance they offer will be at best that of the "partially sighted". (p. 85)

(3) The ethical thinking and teaching found in other Christian Churches

The ethical writings of theologians outside the Roman Catholic Church were hardly mentioned in the moral theology I studied in the seminary. That was not the case when I pursued my post-graduate work at Fribourg University. There I discovered a very rich vein of moral theology in the Anglican Caroline divines of the seventeenth century. In fact, I found that they were more faithful to the authentic teaching of Aquinas than were many of the Catholic manuals of moral theology, despite their claim to be written 'secundum mentem Sanctae Thomae'.[4]

Today the ecumenical dimension of moral theology is taken for granted. As a Catholic moral theologian, I can honestly say that my appreciation of Christian morality has been greatly enriched by the writings of numerous theologians from other Churches writing in the field of Christian ethics and also by personal contact and friendship with many of them in this country. (I write further on this in tip no. 6 on p. 135 of Chapter 9.)

In 1994 a new, challenging and enriching resource was published. The Agreed Statement on moral issues by the Second Anglican-Roman Catholic International Commission, *Life in Christ: Morals, Communion and the Church*, is an attempt by two Churches to try to think inside each other's approach to moral issues, both at a general level and with regard to some particular issues which might seem to put these Churches on a collision course. There is no attempt on either side to claim that their approach is the only valid one or that their teaching on this particular issue has a monopoly of the truth. This is a long way from 'the truth, the whole truth and nothing but the truth' of the moral theology I learnt in the seminary. A couple of quotations might help to illustrate the point I am making. They discuss two specific issues on which the two Churches disagree: the first deals with divorce and remarriage, the second with contraception:

> Roman Catholic teaching and law uphold the indissolubility of the marriage covenant, even when the human relationship of love and trust has ceased to exist and there is no practical possibility of recreating it. The Anglican position, though equally concerned with the sacramentality of marriage and the common good of the community, does not necessarily understand these in the same way. Some Anglicans attend more closely to the actual character of the relationship between husband and wife. Where a relationship of mutual love and trust has clearly ceased to exist, and there is no practical possibility of remaking it, the bond itself, they argue, has also ceased to exist. When the past has been forgiven and healed, a new covenant and bond may in good faith be made. (75)
>
> Anglicans understand the good of procreation to be a norm governing the married relationship as a whole. Roman

> Catholic teaching, on the other hand, requires that each and every act of intercourse should be 'open to procreation'...(81) The immediate point at issue in this controversy would seem to concern the moral integrity of the act of marital intercourse. Both our traditions agree that this involves the two basic 'goods' of marriage, love union and procreation. Moral integrity requires that husband and wife respect both these goods together. For Anglicans, it is sufficient that this respect should characterise the married relationship as a whole; whereas for Roman Catholics, it must characterise each act of sexual intercourse. (82) The Roman Catholic doctrine is not simply an authoritative statement on the nature of the integrity of the marital act...The definition of integrity is founded upon a number of considerations: a way of understanding human persons; the meaning of marital love; the unique dignity of an act which can engender new life; the relationship between human fruitfulness and divine creativity; the special vocation of the married couple; and the requirements of the virtue of marital chastity. Anglicans accept all of these considerations as relevant to determining the integrity of the marital relationship and act. Thus they share the same spectrum of moral and theological considerations. (80)

Both these statements seem to be saying something much more significant than that they agree to differ. Before agreeing to differ, they are agreeing that they both hold to the same Christian vision and the same fundamental values which lie at the heart of the issues under discussion. They also seem to be agreeing that the position with which they disagree should be respected as an honest and conscientious attempt to be true to this vision and these values. If that is an accurate reading of these statements, it would seem to suggest that a similar respect should be shown to those within each Church who disagree conscientiously with their own Church's position on these issues.

(4) The explosion of our empirical knowledge and consequent advances in human technology

It is commonplace to say that we have far more knowledge about ourselves as human persons than people in previous ages. We know far more about ourselves as sexual beings at both relational and reproductive levels. We understand much more about the subconscious and the enormous impact experiences in early childhood can have on the human psyche. We are more aware of the many ways in which our human freedom is limited. We have much deeper understanding of the animal dimension to us and also the purely biological and chemical side of our bodies and how this can interact with our minds and emotions. Our understanding of social processes has also increased, even though in economics we still do not seem to know how to control what is happening at a global level. We have also developed complex technologies, especially in the field of communications. All this new knowledge does not necessarily make us wiser people. That would depend on how we use this knowledge.

This is the world in which moral theologians today have to ply their trade. Gone are the days when the moral theologian was able to speak with presumed authority on any and every subject. The kind of knowledge needed for informed comment on many issues is so specialised that many moral theologians are concentrating on very specific fields. For instance, in recent years the leading British moral theologian, Jack Mahoney, limited himself to the field of business ethics and was, until his retirement in September 1998, the first Dixon Professor of Business Ethics at the London Business School. In the field of medical ethics, some moral theologians are specialising in particular areas of medicine such as life and death issues, reproductive medicine or genetics. Some are even beginning to specialise in the ethics of advertising or tourism.

Other moral theologians are going in the opposite direction and are focusing their attention on that part of the discipline which used to be called fundamental moral theology. In other words, they are concentrating more on what are called metaethical questions. These are issues which have a bearing right across the board in all areas of life: How do we go about moral decision-making? What is the role of conscience? Where does authoritative Church teaching come in and what are the legitimate parameters of legitimate response to it? How do we handle our moral beliefs in a pluralist society? Can a civilised society exist without some kind of agreed common morality? What are the basic principles or values of such a common morality and how are they grounded? The list of such questions is endless. However, moral theologians are not reinventing the wheel. Our human family has been wrestling with these or similar questions down through the ages. As mentioned earlier, we are like dwarfs standing on the shoulders of giants. Perhaps one important role for moral theology today is to make sure that the wisdom of the giants is fed into the contemporary debate.

(5) Historical consciousness

Formerly history tended to be looked on as the study of the past. Today it is seen as a dimension of the present. We are essentially historical persons. We are shaped by our past. The kind of person we become is greatly influenced by our personal, family, neighbourhood, ethnic and national histories. The same is true at Church level. Vatican II was not a rejection of our history and tradition. It was a rediscovery of the vitality and dynamism of our living tradition through recovering a sense of historical consciousness. There is a paradox about a living tradition, as Newman pointed out. It needs to change if it is to maintain its true identity. Kevin Nichols puts it well: 'If it fails to do this [i.e. 'change in order to remain the same'], its formulations turn into relics, fixed and dead, like flies elegantly preserved in amber.'[5]

Historical consciousness also challenges the notion of 'the truth, the whole truth, and nothing but the truth'. Without going down the blind alley of relativism, moral theologians today need to be conscious that any formulation of moral truth is historically conditioned. It will have been crafted and refined in the course of historical debates, often arising from a consideration of particular moral problems that have arisen at a certain point in time. In a sense, down through the ages, within its own particular historical context, it is always struggling with the same question – what is the meaning of being human in the light of the best self-understanding of our age and what are the implications of this in real life. Sometimes the process of struggling with that question works in reverse. Practical ethical decisions have to be made, often without time for long and protracted reflection. That comes later. If a decision has had to be made 'on the hoof', as it were, our conviction that this was the right decision leads us to reflect later about what this says about how we understand ourselves as human persons. Jack Mahoney captures this process very succinctly when he describes it as 'trying to make faith-sense of experience and at the same time of making experience-sense of faith'.[6]

The basic structures of human life and social relations, marriage, even gender and sexual orientation, have not dropped down fully formed from heaven. They are human artefacts in the sense that human beings have found these patterns of living and relating as necessary if they are to do justice to themselves as human persons. These basic institutions are natural in the sense that human beings have discovered them by looking at themselves as human persons. Yet that same process of self-discovery continues to be ongoing throughout history. Moreover, it always takes place in a cultural context. Though basic human institutions such as these may be fundamental to human living, that does not mean that their present form is carved on stone and completely unalterable. They have been shaped by our forebears in the light of their best self-understanding. We have the responsibility to be faithful to this continuing task they have passed on to us. Therefore, if new knowledge or experience teaches us that aspects of these basic institutions need to be re-formed in any way, we would be failing in our God-given responsibility if we refused to accept this challenge. Such a position is fully in keeping with a dynamic interpretation of natural law thinking since it is the only way we can be true to the God-given gift of ourselves as human persons.[7]

(6) Human experience

The total rejection of artificial contraception by Paul VI in *Humanae Vitae* came as a shock to me. I had expected him to follow the kind of approach proposed by the Papal Birth Control Commission, which offered a theological breakthrough along the lines of the Anglican position as explained in the first ARCIC quotation on pp. 118–9. It argued that the human (and, therefore, moral) significance of individual sexual acts should be interpreted in the light of their place within the relationship as a whole. Consequently, an individual act of sexual intercourse which was contraceptive in a purely *physical* sense could still be seen as *morally* procreative (i.e. life-giving). That would be the case if the couple's relationship itself was open to life and if this act served that life-giving relationship by helping to heal, sustain and increase the couple's life-giving love. That love is essential for their life-giving mission as parents since it awakens in their children that sense of security and self-acceptance which is needed if they are to grow more fully alive as loving human persons.

Probably due to a defective ecclesiology on my part (or maybe because I am not a naturally confrontational person), my initial reaction to *Humanae Vitae* was: 'I now need to sit down and think again. The Pope's act of teaching in this encyclical is an ecclesial action I cannot simply ignore. I need to be open to the possibility that the Holy Spirit is giving the Church some new insight in this encyclical or, better, helping us to see old truths in a new way.' A series of four articles I wrote in *The Clergy Review* in 1972 was part of my going through that process. However, what finally convinced me that the Papal Birth Control Commission's position was a richer presentation of Catholic moral understanding than the Pope's encyclical was the fact that the latter failed to speak to the experience of most Catholic married couples. I could tell lots of stories to illustrate that point but one in particular stands out in my mind.

I was giving a talk to a large gathering of couples in the north of England. They were extremely committed Catholic couples who regularly each month met together in small groups for prayer and reflection. They would help each other look honestly at their lives and try to discern God's call to them in the events of their daily living. I did my level best to present the teaching of *Humanae Vitae* in a positive and attractive way to them. Towards the end of the meeting I asked them to help me by filling in a questionnaire which asked for their own reactions to the encyclical and how it touched them in their lives. Their response was an eye-opener for me. It was clear that what *Humanae Vitae* had to say about contraception simply did not speak to their experience as committed Catholic couples. For them the reasons given for the Church's prohibition were out of tune with their own lived experience of marriage and the ruling itself offered them no practical help. I remembered that experience years later when I read the following passage by Jack Mahoney:

> In the case of *Humanae Vitae* ... Pope Paul may appear to imply that the reception of his teaching by the Church at large will have, through the complementary influence of the Spirit, at least a confirmatory value in establishing the truth of his teaching. The possibility cannot be ruled out, however, that in such non-infallible teaching on a matter which is not contained in revelation the response of the body of the faithful will be less than whole-hearted in agreeing with the papal teaching and the considerations underlying it. For the influence of the Holy Spirit in the hearts of the faithful, as described by Pope Paul, is envisaged purely as disposing them to be receptive, whereas it might be a more positive one of refining, qualifying, or even correcting the papal teaching.[8]

(7) Dialogue

The need for dialogue flows from our renewed self-understanding as Church. We have to be a learning Church as well as a teaching Church. If we are to learn, we have to share in dialogue with those who see life somewhat differently from ourselves. Such conversation is not focused on convincing them that they are wrong. It starts from the belief that we have riches to share with them and that, almost certainly, they too have riches to share with us. Hence, dialogue is not just about speaking. Listening is an essential ingredient to dialogue.

For moral theologians today dialogue must be part of our trade. We have to dialogue with other disciplines so that we can better understand ourselves and the world we are living in. We have to dialogue with other Churches so that we can mutually enrich each other about the moral implications of the faith we share. We have to dialogue with other faiths since we believe that the wisdom and action of God's Spirit is not locked up within the confines of the Christian faith. Moreover, without this kind of respectful dialogue we cannot expect to get an attentive hearing for the riches we believe we can contribute to our partners in conversation.

Dialogue is also necessary within our own Catholic community. Sadly, it is here that dialogue is sometimes most difficult. Our Catholic community seems to have a curious blind spot in this regard. We are prepared to engage in dialogue and even expect some measure of disagreement on issues of social ethics, for instance. An outstanding example of this is the fine pastoral letter on the economy published by the U.S. bishops after an exemplary dialogue process, including the publication of preparatory drafts followed by public hearings and linked to an open invitation for comment. In the final version, the bishops explicitly recognise that, apart from their basic gospel-rooted fundamental principles, people should feel free to disagree with their more specific teachings, provided they are willing to give them a serious hearing:

> 134. In focusing on some of the central economic issues and choices in American life in the light of moral principles, we are aware that the movement from principle to policy is complex and difficult and that although moral values are essential in determining public policies, they do not dictate specific solutions. They must interact with empirical data, with historical, social and political realities, and with competing demands on limited resources. The soundness of our prudential judgements depends not only on the moral force

of our principles, but also on the accuracy of our information and the validity of our assumptions.

> 135. Our judgements and recommendations on specific economic issues, therefore, do not carry the same moral authority as our statements of universal moral principles and formal church teaching; the former are related to circumstances which can change or which can be interpreted differently by people of good will. We expect and welcome debate on our specific policy recommendations. Nevertheless, we want our statements on these matters to be given serious consideration by Catholics as they determine whether their own moral judgements are consistent with the Gospel and with Catholic social teaching . . .[9]

The strange thing is that such a warm invitation to dialogue and openness to the possibility of disagreement is not deemed acceptable in matters of sexual ethics or bioethics. This anomaly makes life particularly difficult for moral theologians since many of the issues which crop up in public debate are precisely in those two areas of ethics.

(8) Involvement in the public arena and media exposure

If moral theology is to be in tune with the spirit of our modern age, it can no longer confine its discussions to behind closed doors or the privileged pages of some inaccessible theological journal. Moral questions are the constant topic of open debate in the media. Moral theologians today are forced to make a choice. They can refuse to play any part in this public debate. While such a choice might give them a quiet life and remove them from any tension with the Vatican or their local hierarchy, it would seem to be an evasion of their ministry as moral theologians in the Church and the world. On the other hand, they can choose to involve themselves in the thick of the debate. This second choice will commit them to abide by the rules of dialogue, which means that they must be prepared to say what they honestly believe. Obviously, they can, and usually should, report the authentic teaching of the Church, since that is part of the contribution they are expected to make. However, they must also be prepared to be critical of that teaching to the extent that it is open to serious theological questioning. To evade such a critical stance when it is demanded by sound theological scholarship would be to surrender one's credibility in the dialogue. Moreover, it would also harm the credibility of the Church's commitment to truth. Most people would assume that such an evasive stance by a moral theologian was due to fear of some kind of disciplinary action on the part of Church authorities.

The American bishop, James Malone, highlights the importance of openness and honesty on the part of theologians and bishops involved in debate in the public arena:

> Bishops and theologians must manage our collaboration and our conflicts on center stage: we should face this fact. . .A democracy lives by open, public debate where all parties are both free to speak and accountable for the implications of their positions. . .Catholicism is not a democracy; but that truism does not touch the question of how Catholicism lives in a democratic culture. . . Bishops and theologians must preserve the faith and share the faith in a culture which values the courage of convictions openly stated, openly criticized and openly defended. . .[There is need for] a teaching style which fosters within the Church and with the wider society what Father Murray called 'civilized conversation'. . .The cultivation of such civil discourse between bishops and theologians should be a model for extending the same dialogue into church and society.[10]

When moral theologians participate in public dialogue in this way, especially when their contribution involves questioning some aspects of official teaching in the light of scientific and historical analysis, understandably this can becomes an occasion for tension between them and Church authorities. However, as long as these moral theologians are motivated by a real love for the Church and concern for its mission and the integrity of its teaching and as long as they do not reject the authority of the Church authorities to give moral teaching, their constructively critical contribution to the public dialogue should be interpreted as an attempt to help rather than hinder the Church in the exercise of its teaching ministry.

For many people strong moral leadership is what the Church should be giving today. Moreover, a clear, unambiguous and strongly authoritative statement on some moral issue is much more likely to attract the attention of the media than a statement hedged about by various qualifications. The media will be even less interested if such a qualified statement is claiming to be no more than a contribution to an ongoing dialogue and one that is open to further revision. Yet such a qualified statement is often what many moral theologians would advocate. Consequently, they can sometimes give the impression of being disloyal to the Church and of sabotaging its clear moral witness when they question some of the strong and unambiguous public moral statements made by Church authorities.

Moral theologians who find themselves in this situation are in a dilemma. They can appreciate the need for a strong lead on moral issues but at the same time they see their questioning reaction as the only appropriate response they can offer if they are to be true to the service they are called to give within and for the Church. Their stance does not arise from any lack of respect for the Vatican or the bishops nor from any denial of their right to speak on behalf of the Church. Rather, they feel obliged to voice their criticism precisely because they believe that the statement in question is not doing justice to the richest moral insights within the Church and may even be misleading as a guide to practical moral action. They are virtually saying that they believe that the Church has richer and more life-giving teaching to offer the world than is contained in this statement.

On some occasions they may also feel a sense of obligation to lay-people in the Church who are not moral theologians and who may still be looking to them for some sort of moral guidance. For instance, in the case of in-vitro fertilisation, at least when the sperm and ovum are from the married couple themselves, should a moral theologian maintain a respectful silence if he or she believes that the Congregation of the Doctrine for the Faith's rejection of this procedure is erroneous and fails to take account of the best moral thinking both within the Catholic Church and among Christians as a whole? Has a moral theologian no responsibility towards the infertile couple who are longing for a child of their own and who are struggling to arrive at a conscientious decision on this issue and who may find the official teaching incomprehensible. The same may be true with regard to the issue of contraception in general or the use of condoms in a particular situation when one partner is at risk of HIV-infection from the other.

When a new and difficult ethical issue comes up in the public forum, the media are always keen to know what is the position of the Catholic Church on this question. Any public statement issued as a reply to that question, if it is to be adequate, needs to be formulated in the light of the best moral thinking that the Church can draw on. This means that there needs to be adequate consultation to ensure that the statement has benefited from a thorough theological analysis. That will not happen if, as often seems to be the case, only one school of moral thinking has been listened to and especially if that school is not representative of the majority of moral theologians. A moral statement which is the result of truly broad-based consultation and dialogue is far more likely to be received positively by moral theologians since its intrinsic authority is likely to be greater. Also, it will probably be more comprehensible and of greater practical benefit to believers and non-believers alike.

(9) Positively critical conversation with a Pope-theologian

The present Pope is a philosopher of repute who has also involved himself in the field of moral theology. One result of this is that, more than previous popes, he is inclined to 'do moral theology' in public. Also, he probably involves himself much more personally in the composition of Vatican statements on moral issues. This creates a dilemma for some moral theologians. Although they may feel a personal admiration and even affection for the Pope similar to that of many fellow Catholics, they know that they must not let this interfere with the service they owe the Church and its mission in their role as moral theologians. Consequently, there may be times when their responsibility as moral theologians obliges them to adopt a critical stance towards some of the moral teaching of the Pope or the moral argumentation he might use to ground such teaching.

To remain silent from a misguided respect for the Pope could actually contribute to what Richard McCormick describes as a 'weakening of the papal magisterium'. McCormick's warning to bishops applies equally to moral theologians:

> If bishops are not speaking their true sentiments, then clearly the pope is not able to draw on the wisdom and reflection of the bishops in the exercise of his ordinary magisterium. When this happens, the presumption of truth in papal teaching is weakened, because such a presumption assumes that the ordinary sources of human understanding have been consulted, as the late Karl Rahner so repeatedly argued. That is why what is called the "enforcement of doctrine" is literally counter-productive. It weakens the very vehicle (papal magisterium) that proposes to be the agent of strength and certainty.[11]

It is sometimes suggested that for the sake of the internal unity (*communio*) of the Church, moral theologians should be prepared to accept the discipline of a 'reverential silence' rather than voice their disagreement in the public forum. How far such an attitude of 'reverential silence' was appropriate in the past is open to debate. I would suggest that it is rarely appropriate today. I agree with Karl Rahner's statement that our contemporary society 'makes such *silentium obsequiosum* quite impossible to maintain any longer'.[12] It could even be argued that, in today's climate of public openness and accountability, for a moral theologian to maintain a 'reverential silence' would leave him or her open to the charge of professional irresponsibility.

Conclusion

Maybe I could finish by giving a brief indication of a few other ways in which moral theology today has changed – or needs to change:

- We are living in a 'time' (*kairos*) of AIDS and our global response, as Christians and world-citizens, to this pandemic is a major moral challenge facing our Christian Churches and our human family.[13]
- Moral theology in the context of Britain today needs to explore the ethical implications of being a nation still grappling with post-Thatcherism, inextricably (I hope) bound up with Europe, living in a global economy and facing the co-responsibility of being part of a world in which the gap between rich and poor (internationally and intra-nationally) is nothing short of criminal.
- The development of a solidly based and well-informed ecological ethics is a matter of major importance since a moral theology which fails do full justice to this is also failing to do justice to the nature of the human person, integrally and adequately considered.
- Moral theology needs to face the media's enormous potential for good and its fearful power for manipulation, exploitation and distortion of the truth.
- There are many ways in which modern information technology, despite its dangers, can help moral theology by facilitating distance learning and discussion and by making information needed for informed moral judgement and debate more accessible.
- Contemporary Old and New Testament scholarship reminds moral theology that it will be under-nourished biblically if it ignores the culture-gap between the Bible and our own age. Two symptoms of such under-nourishment would be trying to equate biblical morality (or moralities) with Christian morality or using biblical quotations as proof texts to answer contemporary moral problems.

I am in no doubt that Richard Niebuhr's sermon title, 'The

Shaking of the Foundations', is an apt description of what has been happening in moral theology in recent years. I thank God for the grace-filled privilege of living through the 'moving' experience of the Spirit-inspired Second Vatican Council with its 'foundation-shaking' impact on moral theology. Moral theology certainly has a very different face to the one I first encountered in my seminary studies in the fifties. Nevertheless, though being a moral theologian has its share of headaches, it has more than its share of consolations.

9

Life in Christ: the Moral Teaching of the Catechism of the Catholic Church

In their statement issued on 20 November 1992 the bishops of England and Wales described the Catechism as 'a tool to aid and guide those who are responsible for teaching the faith'. This suggests that the Catechism has been written primarily for bishops, clergy and religious educators in general. However, the fact that it has sold so well in bookshops, religious and secular, would suggest that its readers extend far beyond specialists in religious education. Moreover, in later statements the same bishops, both collectively and individually, have encouraged all Catholics to read it. Sometimes tools intended for specialists can be dangerous for non-specialists to handle. It is possible that this could be the case with Part III of the Catechism which deals with the Roman Catholic Church's moral teaching. Our bishops have expressed the hope that reading the Catechism might help people 'enter more deeply into the mysteries of God's love and life'. The following rather tentative tips are offered to non-specialist readers of Part III in the hope that they might further this purpose.

When the English-language version of *The Catechism of the Catholic Church* was published in 1994, I wrote two articles to help ensure that its readers were able to draw positive inspiration from what it said about morality rather than being demoralised by certain aspects of its approach to Christian morality. 'The Catechism & moral teaching: 10 tentative tips for readers', appeared in *The Month*, 1994, pp. 266–9 and 'The spirit and the letter' was published in *The Tablet*, 4 June 1994, pp. 722–3. This chapter is based substantially on the article in *The Month*. However, I have supplemented it with parts of the article in *The Tablet* where this seemed appropriate.

1. Part III of the Catechism will only be understood properly if read within the wider context of the Catechism as a whole. That context is essentially relational. The first two parts of the Catechism spell out who we are in relation to God as revealed to us in the person of Christ. Part III, with its all-important heading 'Life in Christ', is aimed at helping us to be/become who we are, recognising that we profess our faith through the way we actually live our lives.
2. In reading the text do not overlook the headings. A few years ago I was asked to give a talk on what the Catechism has to say about morality. The organisers did not notice that the overall title of Part III is 'Life in Christ'. Hence, they billed my talk as 'The Ten Commandments'! If we overlook the relationship between the headings and subheadings in the Catechism, we may easily miss the wood for the trees.
3. Do not read the two sections of Part III as two equal and separate halves to be seen in isolation from each other. The first section, entitled 'Man's Vocation: Life in the Spirit' (the original inclusive language translation read 'The Human Vocation: Life in the Spirit'), lays down the underlying spirit and basic principles which should colour our reading of the second section, 'The Ten Commandments'. Unless this is done, there is a danger that the teaching contained under these commandments will no longer be life-giving but will be reduced to legalistically interpreted, purely human rules. Some people will feel self-justified with their high level of performance, while others whose life-possibilities are reduced by a variety of enormous pressures or those who find that scrupulous fidelity to the letter of the law often stifles the spirit, will feel despised and condemned.
4. Interpret the Ten Commandments as drawing out the implications of the twofold command to love God and love our neighbour. The Catechism stresses this point very emphatically and, in so doing, is faithful to the earliest Christian tradition. Consequently, we should presume we are misunderstanding the practical implications of the decalogue if we interpret any of them to be demanding behaviour which is clearly dehumanising and violates the good of human persons. To make us more sensitive to this

way of reading the Ten Commandments readers might find the following exercise helpful. Write a positive version of the Ten Commandments in the language of the twofold commandment of love, bringing out the human values highlighted in each commandment. In the appendix to this chapter I have tried this exercise myself, based on how the Catechism itself has tackled each of the commandments.

5. Part III of the Catechism, like the Pope's encyclical, *Veritatis Splendor*, presents Catholic moral teaching in the light of Vatican II. Both documents state this very explicitly. Hence, any reading of either of these documents which turns the clock back on Vatican II must be rejected as a misinterpretation. One way to avoid any such misinterpretation might be to refresh one's appreciation of Vatican II's approach to morality by rereading its major contribution to this field, the *Pastoral Constitution on the Church in the Modern World.*
6. Since Vatican II, any presentation of the Catholic faith must have an ecumenical dimension to it. This entails more than a longing for the unity for which Christ prayed. It also involves a recognition that God's Spirit is at work in other Christian Churches. It is in this spirit that the moral section of the Catechism needs to be read. This implies that, when there are particular issues of moral disagreement between the major Christian Churches, the Catechism's presentation of the current authoritative Catholic teaching should not be presumed to be the final and definitive Christian position on this topic. The Catechism offers a helpful ecumenical service in presenting an authoritative Catholic position. However, it would be ecumenically harmful if such a presentation was understood to carry such authority that any other position must be rejected as unchristian. The importance of this point was brought out all the more through the publication in 1994 of *Life in Christ, an Agreed Statement by the Second Anglican-Roman Catholic International Commission (ARCIC II)*. This agreed statement is a powerful witness to the fact that, even on those specific moral issues where these two Churches disagree, they still share the same vision and are committed to the same common values. Over the past few years, very interesting work has been done at the World

Council of Churches in the field of ecumenism and ethics. Much of it has been published in *The Ecumenical Review* between 1995 and 1997. Of particular interest to Catholic readers is the study document produced by the Joint WCC-RC Working Party, *The Ecumenical Dialogue on Moral Issues: Potential Sources of Common Witness or of Divisions*.[1]

7. A similar point to the one made in the previous section needs to be stated with regard to those occasions when the Catholic Church's moral teaching is in conflict with the deeply-held moral convictions of most ordinary good-living men and women, be they Christian or not. This is not suggesting that moral truth can be reduced to a majority vote. Rather, it is based on a fundamental insight of Vatican II, which is reflected in the title of Part III, Part I of the Catechism, 'The Human Vocation: Life in the Spirit'. Every human person who is open to the call of the transcendent in life and who responds respectfully and unselfishly to the other, and his or her needs as encountered in life, is being moved by God's Spirit. As Schillebeeckx says, a Church attentive to the prompting of God's Spirit will listen to 'foreign prophecy' coming from outside its own ranks.
8. While readers skilled in biblical exegesis might be put off by the frequent uncritical use of biblical passages in the Catechism, others might find its quasi-devotional use of the Bible and other Christian sources inspirational and helpful for prayerful reflection. However, they should not see such use of Scripture and tradition as having any probative force in validating the teaching in question. This is all the more important in the case of issues still under debate in the Catholic Church or between Christians.
9. Readers may look to the Catechism for help in forming their consciences. Christian tradition has always tried to keep a balance between two fundamental truths about conscience. One is the primacy of conscience, and flows from the fact that, as moral agents, we have to accept responsibility for our own decisions. We cannot shift responsibility to anyone else, not even the Church or the Pope and the bishops. Ultimately we have to follow our conscience. That remains true even when it is in error. The second truth about con-

science is implied in the very word itself. Literally conscience means 'knowing-with'. As interdependent and social persons we cannot undertake our search for moral truth in splendid isolation. Our Christian faith with its focus on the relational and community dimensions of life serves to emphasise this point. Moreover, the faith we share in common is not some esoteric belief divorced from everyday life. It has to be made flesh in the practical reality of our interpersonal and social lives. To claim that the gospel has no relevance for daily life is to deny an essential dimension of our Christian faith. This means that the Church is acting within its proper field of competence when it offers teaching on moral issues. For those of us who are Catholics, implicit in what is meant by a Catholic Christian conscience is that we must listen attentively to the authoritative moral teaching of the Pope and the bishops. Naturally, both these truths about conscience are emphasised in the Catechism. However, it would have been more helpful if the Catechism had reminded readers that these two truths have to be held together in creative tension and are not in conflict with each other. To insist on due respect for authoritative Church teaching is quite different from expecting Catholics to practise blind obedience. The normal presumption in favour of the truth of authoritative moral teaching is no more than a presumption. On occasion serious reasons may lead a Catholic respectfully to qualify this presumption in favour of judging that a particular piece of moral teaching is inadequate, unsatisfactory or even, on occasion, in error, or at least needing radical revision. Disagreement with a particular piece of moral teaching is not tantamount to a denial of the authority of the Pope and bishops to teach on moral issues.

10. The full story of the rejection of the inclusive language translation of the Catechism may never be revealed in the public arena. I have the impression that, notwithstanding some undeniable improvements in the new translation, the whole affair smacks of manipulation by some highly organised and well-funded reactionary pressure groups together with collusion on the part of those with ultimate responsibility for the Catechism. If this impression is correct, it is ironical that a

document in which Catholic moral teaching features so prominently should itself have been subject to immoral manipulation. However, as I pointed out in Chapter 6, our love for the Church needs to be realistic. Hence, we should not look on Church officials, no less than ourselves, as immune from sin and its effects. Consequently, we should not be too surprised if the composition of the Catechism is affected by this, just as it will be affected by the misjudgements and limitations of those who have carried the heavy responsibility for its composition. To recognise the Catechism as authoritative is quite compatible with acknowledging its obvious imperfections. As Spirit-filled believers, we should respect the Catechism. However, equally as Spirit-filled believers, we should also respect our own critical reactions if, on certain moral issues, we find the substance or formulation of what the Catechism says alien to our personal experience of 'life in Christ'.

11. In recent years it has become increasingly recognised that the experience and reflection of women have not been adequately represented in the field of moral theology and in the process of formulating moral teaching in the Catholic Church. This situation is slowly beginning to change. Perhaps the publication of the Catechism offers women another opportunity to bring about change in this regard. For instance, groups of Catholic women could make an in-depth study of Part III of the Catechism, exploring how far its presentation of morality as 'life in Christ' corresponds with the way they experience 'life in Christ' precisely as women. It could be a most enriching experience for the Church to listen to their findings.

It might be helpful to supplement the above 'tips' for reading the moral section of the Catechism with a few observations on its handling of some specific moral issues:

- As one would expect, the Catechism repeats the post-Vatican II teaching of *Humanae Vitae*. However, it does not mention the post-Vatican II phenomenon of the 'non-reception' of the teaching of *Humanae Vitae* by very many Catholic married couples. Hence, the reader is not alerted to the possibility that, through this non-reception, the Holy Spirit might conceivably be leading the Catholic Church to a more satisfactory revision of its teaching on this issue.

- The Catechism's treatment of divorce seems to give the unfortunate impression that moral fault can be presumed to be the major cause of marriage breakdown. This hard-line approach is hardly 'life-giving' to those who have suffered this tragedy in their lives. It is in stark contrast to the approach of the bishops of England and Wales which has been far more sensitive in this regard. The Catechism also uses a much more negative formulation than is usually found in official Catholic statements when it describes remarriage after divorce as 'public and permanent adultery' (n. 2384).
- Its treatment of euthanasia seems to leave open the issue of withdrawing nutrition/hydration to persistent vegetative patients like Tony Bland. While it says that the ordinary care due to a sick person cannot legitimately be interrupted, it also warns against 'over-zealous' treatment and states that 'no one is obliged to continue medical procedures that are unnecessarily burdensome, dangerous, extraordinary or disproportionate to the hoped-for results' (n. 2278).
- Its treatment of homosexuality seems to be deliberately set in a positive context. It is found within the section headed 'Vocation to Chastity'. Moreover, although this section contains a subheading 'Offences against Chastity', homosexuality is given its own positively-headed sub-section headed 'Chastity and Homosexuality'. This is significant, since chastity is a positive virtue governing appropriate loving relationships and behaviour in the sexual field.
- Readers of the Catechism might possibly be misled on one point about abortion. An untrained eye would probably understand n. 2272 to mean that every woman who has an abortion and those who assist her are excommunicated. In fact, the canons of the Code of Canon Law referred to in the footnote point in the very opposite direction, since in most instances their conditions for incurring excommunication are extremely unlikely to have been fulfilled.

The real-life demands of 'Life in Christ', as the moral section of the Catechism is called, cannot be read in a book. They are to be found in our encounters with the significant others who are our companions in life. To the extent that the Catechism makes us more aware of who these significant others are, confronting us with our prejudices and widening the horizons of our vision, it will help the growth of the life of Christ in us. Some critics have teased the Catechism for, as they say, 'creating new sins'. They have mentioned such things as drunken or reckless driving (n. 2290) or drug trafficking (n. 2291). In fact, what the Catechism is rightly doing in such instances is helping its readers to be more sensitive to ways in which we can be unloving to our neighbour in the changed circumstances of modern life.

Yet life in Christ is more than increased awareness and a wider vision. It means actually living our lives out of this awareness and vision. As John Paul II insists in *Veritatis Splendor*, the only credible way to profess our faith is in the way we live our lives. The bishops of England and Wales have expressed the hope that reading the Catechism will help people 'enter more deeply into the mysteries of God's love and life'. In other words, they are insisting that the only way the Catechism should be used is as a help to living more fully. To use it as a weapon for witch-hunting fellow Catholics who might have divergent views on moral issues would be to misuse it.

Growth in Christian morality is a process of character formation and putting on the mind of Christ rather than merely absorbing information about moral teaching. The Catechism can contribute to this process but it is far from being at the centre of it. Perhaps our guiding principle for reading the Catechism should be: draw as much benefit from it as we can but do not give it an undue importance in our Christian lives.

Appendix: The Ten Commandments as mediations of love of God and neighbour and their associated fundamental human values

I. YOU SHALL LOVE THE LORD YOUR GOD BY…

1. Recognising your dignity as human persons, created in the image of God, loved by God and invited to respond to his love.

VALUE
giftedness of human person's ability to relate to God

2. Respecting the sacredness of the gift of human language, enabling you to speak of what is most deep and precious in life – the very mystery of God himself, as well as the deepest mysteries of the human person and the rest of God's creation.

VALUE
giftedness of human person's ability to know God

3. Recognising that nothing in creation is more sacred to God than the human person and that, therefore, the sacredness of ritual and communion serve to fulfil a most fundamental need deep in the heart of each human person.

VALUE
giftedness of human person's ability to encounter God in ritual and communion

II. YOU SHALL LOVE YOUR NEIGHBOUR AS YOURSELF BY. . .

4. Recognising that you receive yourselves as gift from your parents, a gift to be shared gratefully and lovingly with others – within your families and in society at large.

VALUE
goodness of family and social relationships

5. Respecting your giftedness and responsibility as embodied persons, endowed with life to be respected and health to be cared for.

VALUE
goodness of life and health

6. Respecting your giftedness and responsibility as sexual persons, endowed with the capacity for faithful and life-giving loving relationships.

VALUE
goodness of human sexuality, enabling us to share life and love

7. Respecting your giftedness and responsibility as social persons, bound together in interdependence on each other and on the rest of creation of which you are stewards.

VALUE
goodness of living together in society, respectful of the integrity of the rest of God's creation

8. Recognising and respecting the gifts of truth and beauty you are privileged to share and continuing the human quest for a deeper understanding of that truth and for a great appreciation of beauty.

VALUE
goodness of truth and beauty and the human pursuit of both

9./10. Seeking to purify your hearts from the twin idols of lust and greed which divorce the human goods of physical attractiveness and material possessions from what gives them value, namely the dignity of the human person.

VALUE
goodness (blessedness) of purity of heart

10

Conscience Formation and Consciousness-raising in the Parish

Many Catholics, especially of an older generation, have been brought up with a wounded and immature conscience. Sadly it is very easy to pass on this impediment to our children. One major feature of this immaturity is the way we view sin, regarding it basically as disobedience, the infringement of God's law. And God's law is made known to us by the Church in a series of positive requirements (e.g. attending Sunday mass) and negative prohibitions (e.g. no artificial contraception, no masturbation, etc.). The result is that our conscience is reduced to the function of a kind of spiritual cash register, marking up all our sins (according to number and gravity) and having no positive role in the task of discovering what we should or should not do.

Discerning the will of God

The biggest weakness in this approach is its impoverishment of something that is very precious to Christian spirituality, namely, the will of God. Genuine spirituality recognises a close link between our deepest desires and the will of God. This is to be expected when we accept that 'the love of God has been poured into our hearts by the Holy Spirit which has been given us' (Rom. 5:5). If we can really get in touch with our deepest selves, we are at the contact point between ourselves and the Spirit of God. This is what *Gaudium et Spes* means when it speaks of conscience as 'the most secret core and sanctuary of a

---

This is an abbreviated version of an article entitled 'Towards an Adult Conscience' which appeared in *The Way*, 1985, pp. 282-93.

person where we are alone with God, whose voice echoes in our depths' (n. 16).

The law approach to conscience is depersonalising. It takes away our individual input into any decision we make; but, even worse, it leaves no room for the Holy Spirit to touch us as persons. The 'will of God' is objectified in laws, principles and the directives of Church authorities. And even the laws and principles lose their soul by being removed from the sphere of ongoing questioning, searching and probing. God's will becomes equated with a static law, whereas it should be the driving force and inspiration in our decision-making process. As St Thomas puts it so beautifully, 'The New Law in its essence is the gift of the Holy Spirit'.[1]

In the legalist approach to God's will, we can feel safe as long as we are doing what authority tells us to do. A deeper understanding of God's will means that if we are listening to the Spirit in the depths of our being, we will constantly be disturbed out of our comfortable security.

I am not saying that legalism was what was actually taught to Catholics. Nevertheless, it is certainly what many older Catholics believe was taught to them and it is what many of them still believe and live by today. What authority says, goes. Obedience is the important attitude. Our conscience is clear if we do what the Church says. And conversely, we feel guilty if, for whatever reason, we have not fulfilled the objective requirements of one of the Church's laws. For instance, it is disturbing how many older Catholics still feel a need for absolution if they have missed mass on Sunday, even if they were ill and unable to leave the house. This is nothing less than an extreme oppression of conscience. A person who operates on this level has a seriously immature conscience.

There can be no liberation from this oppression until a person comes to believe that our Christian God is a loving God and that there is nothing God wants more deeply than our personal and communal good and happiness. Once a person sees God in that light they are able to understand that sin has no other meaning than what is person-injuring (in the narrow or broad sense). God is affected by sin only because human persons are precious to God and the last thing God wants is for persons to be harmed. To paraphrase St Thomas, we offend God only to the extent that we harm ourselves and others.[2]

It follows from all this that we only come to understand what is sinful by gradually discovering what ways of acting are against the true good of human persons. What is good and evil does not flow from some arbitrary 'will of God' but from the very nature of the human person in community. Therefore, if we want to use the phrase 'law of God' or 'God's will', we must remember that we are not referring to divine edicts handed down from on high. Rather we are talking about a growing awareness among humankind as to what really serves the good of human persons and what contradicts that good. Developing this awareness is a momentous task shared by all men and women down through the ages. Each period of history has to face the fresh questions raised by changes in culture, new breakthroughs in human understanding, and a whole variety of scientific and technological developments. The speed of this whole process seems to have accelerated enormously in our day. The nuclear issue, advances in bioethics, the advent of the microchip, etc., etc., are all posing new questions to men and women today. In what direction lies the true good of humankind?

Discernment and dialogue

In facing these questions, the Church has no hot line to God. God's will does not arrive from heaven in diplomatic bags carried by some angelic courier. The Church has to join in the common search, confident that its belief in the human person as loved by God in Jesus, will give it something precious and unique to offer in this human quest for truth in personal and communal living.

Following the example of *Gaudium et Spes*, the Church has to engage in a dialogue with the world; and that is a dialogue from within. The Church does not look in on the modern world from the outside. The men and women who make up the Church today belong to the modern world. They share the same hopes and fears, sorrows and joys.

Dialogue involves listening and speaking. As Church we must listen to and be up-to-date with the best of scientific knowledge and the most recent technological developments. We must also listen to our own instincts through which we can plug into the common sense of humankind. We must listen to other people of good will – and obviously 'good will' is not the exclusive preserve of Catholics or Christians. We must listen to our catholic and Christian tradition. This is mediated to us mainly through the 'conserving' demands of authority complemented by the counter-thrust of theologians as they strive to understand our traditions in their historical context and thereby are in a position to interpret what is their relevance for contemporary faith and life.

Real sharing in dialogue also involves speaking. Some of that speaking can be checking out whether we have listened correctly. The opening paragraphs of *Gaudium et Spes* are virtually the Church saying to the world, 'This is what I hear you saying: have I got you right?' Some speaking involves moving the dialogue on a stage further, and some involves the articulation of our considered judgements or decisions. The latter is crucial, especially in matters of urgency where decisions need to be made and acted upon.

Urgent and pressing decisions face our modern world. Therefore, our dialogue has to come to practical conclusions, judgements have to be made. They must be the best we can do at the time but very often they can only be provisional, open to further refinement and perhaps even revision. To be practical they need to be definite but that does not mean they have to be definitive. A moral theologian whom I respect highly once said that he would love to read a pastoral letter which began 'I may be wrong but...'! We need to have the courage of our convictions. An open mind does not mean a blank mind devoid of any convictions, but we do need to see ourselves involved in an ongoing search for truth. That does not mean jettisoning the truth we have already attained but it might mean re-examining and rethinking that truth so that we can appreciate its richness even more fully in the light of where we stand today in the ongoing story of human culture and civilisation. The whole of *Gaudium et Spes* is written in this spirit but nowhere is it more clearly expressed than in n. 44 of that Constitution. After speaking about this whole process of dialogue, it then states: 'In this way, revealed truth can always be more deeply penetrated, better understood, and set forth to greater advantage'.

This dialogue process in the Church's involvement in the search for truth throws light on how the individual Christian moves towards a conscience-decision. I use the phrase 'conscience-decision' deliberately. Conscience is not some inner voice telling me what I should do, a kind of hot line to God. Neither is it a negative alarm signal which goes off when I am about to do something wrong. Put very simply, conscience is myself deciding what I should do if I am to respond fully to God in this situation facing me. And responding fully to God implies responding fully to life and to my own deepest level of being.

If we view conscience in this way, it is clear why our understanding of what is meant by 'the will of God' is so important and why we need to be freed from voluntaristic and depersonalising interpretations of God's will. In a sense we create God's will; or better, God's will takes shape through our decisions. We are not puppets, with the whole of our lives and everything we do already pre-programmed by God, the puppet-master. As each major decision looms before us in life, God's will is not already determined and filed away in some kind of divine computer programme. Discovering God's will is not a matter of discovering what God has already decided that we should do. Rather, discovering God's will lies in ourselves deciding what is the most loving and responsible thing for us to do. We discover God's will by actually bringing it into being.

I have always been fond of Charles de Foucauld's prayer of abandonment. Not so long ago I was thrilled to discover just how similar that prayer is to the famous 'Take, Lord, and receive' act of self-offering in the Fourth Week of the Spiritual Exercises. For many years, God forgive me, I had tended to interpret abandonment to God's will in a kind of fatalistic sense. God's will came to me mainly from the outside in the events of life and in the directives and instructions of my bishop and other legitimate authorities. I did not naturally link abandonment to God's will with what my deepest self really wanted to do.

Bit by bit I came to realise that it was meaningless to say to the Lord, 'I offer you my mind and will', and then not use these precious faculties. That was not giving God my mind and will at all: it was simply ceasing to use them. That path leads to fatalism or totalitarianism or to our becoming mere automatons. So it gradually dawned on me that abandonment to God's will was very closely linked with having the faith and courage to respond actively, not passively, to the situations in life. It meant being prepared to make decisions myself and accepting responsibility for my own decisions.

Naturally I am not suggesting that at every moment of the day we are always engaged in important conscience-decisions. Most of the time we are living out of decisions previously made and any intermediate decisions we make may not be of great moral significance, rather like a walker continuing on a path already decided upon. However, sadly, we sometimes find ourselves living without much sense of direction at all and so we experience a lot of what we are doing as pointless, i.e. lacking point or direction.

All this highlights the importance of a traditional Catholic practice which is often misunderstood and in its mistaken form becomes oppressive rather than liberating. That is the daily examination of conscience. Many of us have been taught to view our daily *examen* as a looking back over the day to see in what ways we have sinned. A truer version of it, and one more in keeping with its Ignatian inspiration, sees it as a time for deepening awareness in the busy and humdrum turmoil of daily life – almost an examination of consciousness. It is not a time when we make momentous new conscience decisions. It is more a time for sharpening our awareness of how the ordinary contacts and happenings of our day have this deeper layer to them. They are not pointless. They have all been potential encounter-points with God 'in whom we live, and move, and have our being.' They fit into (or contradict) the purpose of our life as we have determined it to be through our deeper conscience-decisions.

Conscience, guilt and moral blindness

While not wanting to ignore the human phenomenon of guilt, I feel that conscience understood in the way I have just described is light-years away from conscience as reduced to guilt-feelings. That is another impoverishment of conscience which fails to take God's commitment to this life seriously.

Guilt has certainly been a Catholic obsession, though less so today. According to this guilt-centred approach, the important thing was to stand 'not-guilty' before God. That was why, at the level of theory, we tended to be very lenient towards an erroneous conscience. After all, if the error was invincible, there was no guilt present. If a person is not guilty, no sin has been committed, so there is no cause for concern.

There were two snags about this approach. One was that it did not work. Somehow our law attitude to morality induced guilt in people whether they were personally responsible for what they did or not. The other snag was even more serious. It bred an attitude which can best be described as 'irresponsibility towards life'. It failed to see how much this life matters in the eyes of God, almost reducing our present life to a kind of waiting-room for eternity, a supporting feature before the main film. The emphasis was on my personal immunity from guilt, my integrity. As long as my conscience was clear, I did not need to worry.

This life matters enormously to God. And above all, how human persons are treated in this life is of paramount importance to God. Strangely enough, God seems well able to cope with guilt especially when it is good, healthy guilt arising from some real evil which a person has perpetrated but for which they are now sorrowfully owning their personal responsibility. The acceptance of such guilt is a major stepping-stone to forgiveness and real forgiveness is a deep experience of love. 'Her sins, her many sins, must have been forgiven her, or she would not have shown such great love' (Luke 7:47).

It is not guilt that poses a problem to God but blindness. It was the blindness of his people that caused Jesus to weep over Jerusalem. It was the blindness of the Pharisees that infuriated Jesus and caused him to use such strong language in an attempt to break down their resistance.

The problem with a guilt-centred conscience is that it can be blind to the very real suffering of other people and it can fail to see how we may be damaging God's world by the way we are living our lives today. By being turned in on itself it can become purely individualistic. *Gaudium et Spes* challenged Christians to leave that kind of conscience behind them. 'Profound and rapid changes make it particularly urgent that no-one, ignoring the trend of events or drugged by laziness, content himself with a merely individualistic morality . . . Let everyone consider it his sacred obligation to count social necessities among the primary duties of modern life, and to pay heed to them' (n. 30).

The vulnerability of a loving God

If God really loves people and wants them to love and respect each other, it matters enormously to God how we treat each other and how we manage the world and universe that we share as our communal home. God is not an impartial and uninvolved judge passing guilty or not-guilty verdicts on people. God is a committed and deeply involved lover to whom the dignity and happiness of each of us is of crucial importance.

A lover is a very vulnerable person since he or she suffers in and through the sufferings of the beloved. In freely creating humankind out of love, God has become very vulnerable. Sometimes we speak of God as the unmoved mover, the changeless one. Though these expressions have a core of truth in them, we can so easily misunderstand and misinterpret them. We can turn God into a being not really affected by what happens on earth, a God expecting absolute obedience but at root invulnerable to the sufferings of humankind. The stoic philosophers had a word for this state, even looking on it as a state of perfection: they called it 'apathy' (the state of being untouched by pain or suffering).

A greater distortion of the God of the Bible and the God of Jesus could hardly be imagined. The Bible is full of feeling words applied to God – love, jealousy, anger, longing, desire, wrath, etc. To apply the word apathy to the God of the Old Testament could hardly be wider of the mark.

The same is true of Jesus – only more so. Jesus hanging on the cross gives the lie to any notion of God being invulnerable. The crucifixion could be called the vulnerability of God.

At the heart of Christian revelation lies the mystery of God's suffering because of us. That is what the figure of Jesus on the cross is saying to us. Through the mind-blowing generosity of freely deciding to love us into existence God has become totally vulnerable because of us.

Paradoxically it is this pain of God, this outraged anger, which is the source of our confidence as Christians. If God shares our pain, what need do we have to worry about the final outcome? This comes through very strongly in Paul's tremendous shout of trust and confidence at the end of chapter 8 of Romans.

As Christians, we are empowered by sharing the outraged anger of God's love. More than that, if we believe, as we must, that God's Spirit is active in the depths of every man and woman, then in truth everyone is offered the gift of being empowered by the outraged anger of God's love. Surely we can say that this lies at the root of all human restlessness about what is wrong and out of gear and inhuman in our world. Pope Paul is virtually saying that when he writes: 'Beneath an outward appearance of indifference, in the heart of everyone there is a will to live together as brothers and sisters and a thirst for justice and peace which is to be expanded' (*Octogesima adveniens*, 1971).

The cross is the symbol of the pain of God. But the voice of the pain of God in every age – and therefore in our own age also – is the voice of the poor, the oppressed, the weak, the sick, those who are pushed out on to the margins of society. The parable of the Good Samaritan (Luke 10:29–37) and the tableau of the Last Judgement (Matt. 25:31–46) both have the same message for us – we hear the call of God in the cry of the person in need.

Hearing the pain of our world

The voice of the pain of God in our world today is still the voice of the poor, the oppressed, those who are discriminated against, those who are pushed to the edges of our society, those who are always at the back of the queue. The Vatican Council gives voice to the cry of some of these when it denounces all forms of discrimination 'whether based on sex, race, colour, social condition, language or religion'. The voice of the pain of God can be heard at a global level – but the same voice is also to be heard in our neighbourhood, on our street, at work with us, or more probably not at work with us. In fact, the more sensitive we become to it, the more it becomes a deafening chorus – until as individuals we can be overwhelmed by it.

But we do not hear it alone – we must not hear it alone. As a family, whether in the Church or in society, we must listen to it together. And if we hear it in that context of our shared strength in the Church or in society, then far from overwhelming us, this cry of pain can become a challenge and an invitation.

Being a cry for a more fully human life, it is God's voice calling us into the future, inviting us to take up the challenge to continue creating a more human world. Becoming attuned to this voice is a vital factor in the formation of conscience. A very apt description of this process is 'consciousness-raising'. If the listening process involved in this is really operative in us, then we are talking of an activity which can also be described as prayer. Schillebeeckx would even go so far as to refer to it as a form of mysticism.

There is always the temptation to close our ears to that cry of pain. To the extent that we are not sharers in that pain, to the extent that we want to keep our distance from it and not be disturbed by it, to that extent we want to stay where we are. And so 'where we are' comes to be described as order, standing over against disruption, disturbance, any change that can let that pain infiltrate into our tidy corner of the world.

But to opt for order in that sense is really to love what is dead – it is like a death-wish. It is to deny that human history is alive and that an essential part of its life is this cry for increasing emancipation. To be deaf to that cry is to be deaf to the voice of the living God. Through this cry God is calling us constantly into a more human future.

Of course, we need to be aware that what happens in reality is that often the cry of pain comes to us disguised as an outburst of anger, or resentment, or rebellion. Our natural reaction as individuals, and especially as a Church or as society, is to respond in the same language – anger for anger, rejection for rejection, etc. – or else it is to try to muffle the cry by means of directing attention elsewhere or by tackling the superficial symptoms which are only the tip of the iceberg. We will never receive the gift of sharing another's pain unless we approach the other in love with a real desire to listen and a total absence of judgement and condemnation. A perfectionist, moralistic, over-demanding Church will find it difficult to share the pain of the weak and 'sinful' because such a Church will not give them that sense of security and trust which makes it possible for them really to reveal their pain.

One often hears an appeal today for the Church to give firm moral teaching on something or other. 'Why doesn't the Church take a clear stand on the issue?' people say. To my mind, there are far more people looking to the Church not so much for clear moral principles as for compassion and understanding and the assurance that they are not alone in their pain and in their suffering – and that there are grounds for real hope for them.

Jesus heard the cry of people's suffering and pain. He was angered by the insensitivity of the religious leaders of his day and wept over their hardness of heart. If we are to share his outraged anger, we must not rest satisfied with living on the surface. We too must try to go to the roots of the evils causing pain in our society today.

Getting down to the roots

Developing some points made by John Bennett, an American theologian, in his introduction to the Sodepax Report, *In search of a theology of development* (1969), I would like to offer five suggestions about how we as Christians must go down to the roots if we are to be involved in the process of consciousness-raising.

1. God is involved in humanity in history. He is identified with the whole human race in Christ. Therefore, if we are truly to be the subjects of history, co-creators of history with God, we must get down to the root causes of what is happening in society.
2. Human being are essentially both spiritual and material. They are not souls which can without loss be separated from bodies and from communities. One consequence of this is

that as persons we are very vulnerable to a whole variety of social, environmental and cultural factors which can have a severely detrimental impact on our development as human persons. For instance, lack of nutrition in a child in the first six months can cause irreversible brain damage. If the glory of God is the human person fully alive, such negative influences have to be tackled at their roots.

3. Although God's love is for all men and women, nevertheless he has what could be called a 'strategic' preference for the poor, the oppressed, the underprivileged. If we are to act as instruments for his 'strategic' preference, we need to go right to the roots of their problems.
4. There are social consequences of sin, whether of the sins of individuals or of the sins embodied in social groups. To put it very simply and perhaps rather provocatively, our 'original sin' today (i.e. what is wrong at the roots in our society) will condition the sufferings and temptations of the next generation.
5. As human beings we belong to the worldwide family of God. So we must become conscious of those members of our family who are suffering the most. There is almost a reversal of missionary role here. Instead of our sending out missionaries to preach the word of salvation to the pagans, we need to send out humble listeners who will help us hear the pain of the oppressed. Perhaps they will help us to become more conscious of how much we share responsibility for the evil they are suffering.

Anyone who has read my recent book, *New Directions in Sexual Ethics: Moral Theology and the Challenge of AIDS*, will be very familiar with the line of thinking I have outlined in this chapter. In my opening chapter entitled 'Hearing the Challenge of the AIDS Pandemic' I write:

> The more I have learned about the AIDS pandemic, the more convinced I have become that this pandemic is helping to open our eyes to some implications of the Gospel which until now have only been latent but which today are beginning to be seen as enormously important. The process of

hearing these 'new, yet old' calls of the Gospel is linked to our growing awareness of certain evils which have permeated human life over the centuries and to which as Church we seem to have accommodated ourselves down the ages. Somehow the AIDS pandemic is exposing these evils in their true colours and their horror and destructiveness is becoming clear, if we only have eyes to see with.

In no way am I suggesting that AIDS had been sent by God to open our eyes to these Gospel values. That would be a blasphemous suggestion. AIDS is a human catastrophe of global magnitude and can rightly be described as one of the major evils of our day. Nevertheless, paradoxically, good can come from evil. Just as a fatal air-crash can reveal a dangerous design fault in an aircraft, so the AIDS pandemic seems to be revealing some major flaws in the social construction of man-woman gender roles, in the ethical evaluation of our sexual relationships, in our global approach to social justice, and in the way we handle the creative potential of the present moment.

As Schillebeeckx reminds us, God often speaks to us through the 'contrast experience' of our inhumanity towards each other. The voice of God is heard in the cries of suffering caused by such inhumanity. The AIDS pandemic is making us more attentive to God's voice coming to us through the cries of women living with HIV/AIDS. The 'contrast experience' consists in the denial in practice of their full human equality and in their sexual exploitation. In the midst of the inhumanity of this situation, the cry of God's creative spirit is heard: "Become more truly human". Salvation today is inextricably bound up with hearing this cry. Out of the tragedy of all the suffering and dying of AIDS can come a new step forward in the salvation of our human family. To close our ears to this is to refuse to listen to the Gospel speaking to us today.[3]

11

Saints or Sinners? Towards a Spirituality of Growth Out of Sin

Christian spirituality is about answering the call of Jesus. However, Jesus has said very categorically: 'I have come to call not the just but sinners'.[1] Therefore, it looks as though in some way or other there is an essential linkage between spirituality and our being sinners.

Sometimes spirituality is presented as though it had nothing whatsoever to do with sin. At our baptism we have renounced sin and so it is presumed that sin should play no further part in our lives. Sin is viewed as a regression, something we 'fall into'. Being sinful suggests that we are falling below what is seen as an acceptable standard for Christian and human life. It is hard to reconcile this perfectionist approach with Jesus saying that he has come to call sinners. His words suggest our being called out from our sinfulness, rather than our attempting to live some kind of perfect life free from sin. They would seem to imply that our sinfulness is actually the starting point for our spirituality. In this chapter I would like to approach the linkage between Christian spirituality and our sinfulness from three converging directions. I would like to look at Christian spirituality first of all in terms of its being a life-long growth-process out of our being 'victims of sin', and secondly in terms of its

---

The first two sections of this chapter are an edited version of part of my article 'Sin, Spirituality and the Secular', in *The Way*, 1992, 13–22. The third section is mainly new material and the fourth section incorporates an edited version of part of my article 'The Changing Paradigms of Sin' in *New Blackfriars*, 1989, 489–97.[2]

being a life-long growth process out of our being 'agents of sin'. Thirdly, I would like to grapple with the objection that the notion of 'growth out of sin' seems to imply too negative a starting point for Christian spirituality. Finally, I look at the social and ecological implications of such a spirituality.

(1) Christian spirituality as a person's life-long process of growth out of being a 'victim of sin'

If spirituality is to be viewed as a life-long process of growth out of being a 'victim of sin', the question immediately arises: where does each person find his or her particular agenda for this growth? In other words, how am I to discern what Christ is asking of me, victim of sin that I am?

There is a tendency to answer that question along very individualist lines. Each of us is unique. We are not mass-produced on an assembly line. Consequently, Christ calls each of us as unique persons. Each of us has his or her unique personal vocation. Following out this approach, we try to discern in what special ways each of us is a victim of sin, since it is there that we will discover our own personal woundedness and so our own unique need for healing.

That is fine as far as it goes. However, it does not go nearly far enough. To focus on what is unique about me is to take a very partial and impoverished view of myself as a human person. An absolutely essential dimension of my being a human person is the fact that I am, always have been and always will be bound up in a whole series of relationships of interdependence with other human beings. This has enormous implications for me if I am to arrive at a full diagnosis of where my personal woundedness lies. It means, for instance, that my personal woundedness will be connected to the woundedness of other people. Obviously, this does not mean that we are all wounded in exactly the same way. Nevertheless, it does mean that my personal woundedness will be linked to the woundedness of all the significant others in my life.

Moreover, these significant others in my life will be found

within an ever-widening series of concentric circles – my parents, family, educators, friends, neighbours, etc. Their woundedness is likely to have an impact on me in the various dimensions of my being a human person. For example, how I develop as a sexual and relational being will be affected by the woundedness of the people who are close to me as I am passing through the key developmental stages of my life. A U.S. theologian, Beverly Hildung Harrison, has brought this out very powerfully in speaking of what she calls the 'formidable power' of nurturing:

> ...we have the power through acts of love or lovelessness literally to create one another...Because we do not understand love as the power to act-each-other-into-well-being, we also do not understand the depth of our power to thwart life and to maim each other. That fateful choice is ours, either to set free the power of God's love in the world or to deprive each other of the very basis of personhood and community...
>
> It is within the power of human love to build up dignity and self-respect in each other or to tear each other down...Through acts of love directed to us, we become self-respecting and other-regarding persons, and we cannot be one without the other.[3]

My woundedness will also be influenced by the woundedness of the institutions which form part of my social existence – including the Church. Furthermore, it will also be marked, to a greater or lesser extent, by various forms of social woundedness such as patriarchy, racial prejudice, national and cultural deficiencies, homophobia, ecological insensitivity, my belonging to a developed world whose affluence seems to be irretrievably linked to structures of exploitation, etc.

If some or all of these factors go to make up the way I, as a human person, am a victim of sin, by that same token they should also feature on my personal agenda for 'growth out of being a victim of sin'. In other words, they will constitute the complex medium through which the sinner that I am hears the call of Christ. This means that they will form an essential part of the agenda for my personal spirituality in my ordinary, everyday life.

If all this is true, it means that my growth out of sin cannot be something that I can achieve on my own. Nor, in fact, can it be a growth that takes place in me alone. For instance, where my woundedness is relational, the growth in healing must necessarily be relational too. Likewise, where my woundedness goes back to structural roots, growth towards healing may well demand of me some kind of personal involvement in working for structural reform. Theologically, as I point out in the final section of this chapter, this is a strong argument in favour of the communal celebration of reconciliation. It does not argue from convenience – lack of opportunity for individual confession due to excessive numbers or paucity of confessors – but is based on the essential social dimension of our being sinners and the corresponding social dimension of our healing and reconciliation.

Moreover, as human persons we are 'historical' beings. We are the product of history, we live in the midst of history and we ourselves play our own unique part in fashioning history. History is full of ambiguity. Some opportunities are seized, other are lost. Nevertheless, although Christians do not believe in inevitable progress, they do believe that God's Spirit is present and active wherever true human progress occurs in history.[4] This belief in the Spirit active within history should make us sensitive to 'the signs of the times'. These signs of the times constitute part of the call of Christ to the historical sinful persons that we are. Through them we discern some of the growth out of sin that we are called to be part of in our contemporary world. It is significant that, when Council Fathers at Vatican II turned their attention to what was implied in being a Christian in the world of today, the very first thing they did was to try to interpret the signs of the times.[5] I am convinced that a spirituality cannot be truly Christian today if, for instance, it turns a deaf ear to what the Spirit seems to be saying to us through the voices of so many committed women who are articulating the deep sufferings and injustices inflicted on their sisters by patriarchal institutions, including the Church. The same would seem to be true of the voices of those calling us to a greater ecological awareness and responsibility.

(2) Christian spirituality seen as a life-long growth process out of our being an 'agent of sin'

The way we human beings cause harm is not just to do with the consequences of our actions. It also has to do with ourselves as the agents of these actions. We cannot repeatedly act in an unloving way without becoming unloving persons. This would seem to be where the tragic linkage between being victims and agents of sin is located. If our capacity to act lovingly and justly has been seriously wounded, then that is likely to show in the way we behave towards others. In fact, experience seems to indicate that it is a very short step from being a victim of sin to becoming an agent of sin. This is very understandable. After all, part of the evil of sin in this sense is that it can injure and deform us as persons. That is why healing is such an urgent priority and this healing involves some sort of growth out of the woundedness inflicted on us by sin.

It would seem, therefore, that our growth out of being an 'agent of sin' is necessarily linked to our growth out of being a 'victim of sin'. I believe that is a truth which can have far-reaching implications for pastoral practice. For instance, it implies that Christian spirituality needs to lay much more emphasis on why we cause some of the harm that we do. It needs to recognise the inadequacy and unreality of demanding a massive act of naked will-power ('a firm purpose of amendment') through which we are immediately expected to be able to cease from the wrongdoing we are involved in. Because we are so interdependent, it may well be that, for the present and while other factors remain as they are, it is morally impossible for a person to break free completely from the wrongdoing he or she is involved in. In reality, this is a fact of human life which has always been acknowledged and allowed for by wise confessors, even though they did not have the benefit of our current understanding of just how multi-dimensional and far-reaching our interdependence on each other actually is.

Commenting on the fact that many Christian are experiencing a 'shift to an awareness of collective responsibility for individual sins, and individual responsibility for the collective sin', Monika Hellwig notes that:

> Sin and conversion for these Christians are seen in a new light. The question of imputing guilt, calculating the degrees of culpability of freedom and knowledge, simply does not arise in the consciousness of such Christians. They are concerned with discerning patterns of disorientation in their society and in their own lives, without reference to the question of whom to blame. Instead their focus is on who can make a difference in the sinful situation, how, why, when and where . . .
>
> They feel a certain impatience . . . with a spirituality much preoccupied with the quest for perfection in an introspective fashion. They have an urgent sense that the real agenda of continuing redemption is written on a far larger canvas, and that endless preoccupation with perfecting oneself and eliminating personal faults is petty and irresponsible in face of the terrible and unnecessary sufferings of vast masses of our times . . .[6]

I would interpret Hellwig as saying that it is not for us to judge the culpability or otherwise of people who are involved in what we consider to be wrongdoing. We do not know how minimal may be the personal resources individual people have for coping with the extreme pressures they may be under. Hence, it is not for us to set ourselves up as 'sinless' and demand that these 'sinners' overcome these pressures by an act of will which, for all we know, might be completely outside their personal capacity. Rather, the credibility of our opposition to the wrongdoing these people are involved in will depend, to a large extent, on how far we are committed to identifying and combating the social pressures which might be part of the 'sin' of which these people are 'victims'. Moreover, recognising ourselves to be linked in interdependence with these fellow 'victims of sin', we should perhaps be on the look out for ways in which our own interests might be bound up with the maintenance of these social pressures which result in these people 'sinning' in this way. Any such complicity on our part would reveal our shared 'agency' in their sinning. Maybe the words of Jesus to the accusers of the woman taken in adultery are relevant here: 'Let the one who is without sin cast the first stone.'[7]

An example of a pastoral strategy which would seem contrary to this sobering pastoral principle might be the aggressive targeting by some sections of the pro-life movement in the United States of women entering abortion clinics. It is significant that many of the women who attended Archbishop Weakland's 'listening sessions' on abortion focused on a wide variety of social factors which resulted in many women experiencing enormous pressures to resort to abortion. Among these pressures the Archbishop's report instanced 'economic pressures, increased violence, feminization of poverty, consumerism, a continued male dominated society' and it noted that these pressures weigh most heavily on the increasing numbers of women caught in the poverty trap.[8]

(3) Does 'growth out of sin' imply too negative a starting point for Christian spirituality?

We have seen how we can only hear Christ's call to us to the extent that we accept ourselves as 'sinners'. This means acknowledging that we are both 'victims of sin' and 'agents of sin'. We have also looked at how these two ways in which we are 'sinners' play an important part in setting the agenda for our personal 'spirituality'. This agenda is about our life-long process of growth out of sin.

Growth is a term frequently used in discussions about human development. However, to talk of 'growth out of sin' might jar on some ears. This apparently negative starting point hardly seems in tune with how we envisage the normal processes of human growth. However, if we go back to the etymology of the Greek word for 'sin', '*hamartia*' which means 'missing the mark or the target', we might be able to interpret 'growth out of sin' in a way which is more in keeping with the normal processes of human growth. The word *hamartia* suggests that sin involves missing the point of life. It might help to explore that idea further.

Religious people are often tempted to think in terms of an original paradise from which we are expelled through our sin. This interpretation of the 'Garden of Eden' story in chapter 3 of Genesis overlooks the fact that this story is a myth referring to the present as much as to the past. The origin of sin, as people experience it today and in every age, is not to be found in God but in ourselves as God's creatures. However, Christianity does not look to the Book of Genesis for the heart of its belief. Christianity is essentially a faith centred on the person of Christ in whom the fullness of God's unfolding revelation to us is made flesh. This means that the 'point of life' has only been fully revealed to us in and through Christ. And Christ reveals to us that the 'point of life' is the Kingdom of God. This Kingdom is a 'mystery' in the fullest sense of the word, with such a rich abundance of meaning that we will never exhaust it either in the present age or in the age to come. The Kingdom is something we can have some experience of but which we can never fully comprehend. At times we may be able to say 'This is what the Kingdom of God is like'; but we will never be able to say 'Now I know what the Kingdom of God is all about'. The Good News of the Kingdom challenges us with the promise that being human has within it the potential for living a life far richer than we would ever have imagined possible. Jesus speaks of this abundance of life in the language of knowing and loving, our highest and most personal modes of human experience. In fact, the Bible often uses these two modes of human experience interchangeably. Put in simple gospel terms, the point of human life is found in being known and loved by God and each other, and in knowing and loving God and each other.

That is not the original state from which our first ancestors fell. Nevertheless, it is a dream of which our earliest ancestors seem to have had some inkling. However, the struggle to survive and gradually come to terms with the emergence of communal and social living meant that this dream was little more than a backcloth of hope in the midst of the harsh realities of everyday survival. Yet it was a dream which would not die. The process of evolution into humanness entailed this process of opening out to the transcendent. In God's providence this gave humankind a growing capacity to be open to God's self-revelation. Without such a capacity we would not have been 'human', we would not have been able to grasp the 'point of life' and the Word and Love of God could not have been made flesh among us.

I have been fumbling for words in the above paragraph. That is what happens when one tries to express the inexpressible. Nevertheless, if what I have been trying to say is basically true, however inadequately it is expressed, it throws a totally different light on the expression 'growth out of sin'. No longer does it imply that the starting point of this growth is some God-forsaken place, some kind of morass of evil into which humankind has regressed. It suggests, rather, that the 'point of life' is something towards which humankind as a whole is growing in a life-long process of interdependence – and the expression 'life-long' here refers to the life of the whole human family, not just to the life of single individuals.

Of course, this is not meant to imply a deterministic view of human history. An essential factor in being human is that we are persons with the capacity to make free decisions. Consequently, part of the 'mystery' which constitutes the 'point of human life' is that God's providential designs are and can only be achieved through the instrumentality of human freedom. However much people may believe in God, it pales into insignificance compared to the belief God has in people! In a theological discussion about how we should respond to the Millennium event, the Irish theologian, Enda McDonagh, spoke of the 'risk of God'. His use of that phrase was pregnant with meaning. Part of it was touching on the risk taken by God in the whole process of creation and incarnation and on how that risk follows through into our human and ecclesial task of building the Kingdom of God here on earth and not simply postponing its coming to the end of time.

The 'mystery', which is the 'point of human life', operates at both the macro and the micro level. The macro level is the total history of humankind. The micro level consists in the stories of our own unique personal lives. Here too this 'mystery' perspective enables us to see our 'growth out of sin' in a much more positive perspective. The 'sin' out of which we are growing need not be seen as a mass of unredeemed evil which we have inherited. It is rather the shadow side of our human family's fluctuating struggle to make the dream of the Kingdom a reality in our world.

This struggle is a story of partial success and partial failure, a mixture of heroic self-sacrificing love and narrow-minded self-seeking. It is full of the necessary human conflict involved in trying to make allowance for the conflicting claims of different individuals or groups. Each of us comes on the scene at a particular point in this ongoing story which is so full of ambivalence. Such is the complexity of our interdependence, each of us is affected by both the ebb and flow movements in the different dimensions of our being human persons. In some of these dimensions we may be predominantly 'inheritors of grace'; in others, 'victims of sin' might be a more accurate description of our situation.

This admixture provides the raw material out of which we have to construct our lives. Christ calls us as 'sinners' to receive the gift of this raw material and to live our lives as fully as possible out of this bundle of light and shade. Growth out of sin is merely another way of describing our life-long task of playing our minor but necessary and unique part in the ongoing story of humankind as it continues its struggle to give living shape and substance to the 'point of life' revealed to us in Christ.

This interpretation of spirituality has no room for a perfectionist ethic. It is too solidly based in the God-given reality of the everyday world. There is no such thing as a perfect human being which we are all called to become. In a sense, morality for each of us is a personal affair. That does not mean that it is individualistic, or relative, or something we make up to suit our own convenience. Rather it is personal in the sense that it flows from the person each of us is, 'integrally and adequately considered'. Christ's call to me is to be myself, the person I am, considered in all the different dimensions of human personhood. Whether my response to this invitation is one of acceptance or rejection will be revealed in my life. The way I live my life constitutes my faith-response to God. That is true of every person who has ever lived.

This spirituality takes on board the fact that as we gradually come to self-awareness, we discover that the person we are growing into, due to the influence of others and our own reaction to their influence, is not as fully human as we might like. The dawning of this self-understanding can offer us the opportunity for entering into the life-long process of personal healing. Accepting as gift the wounded person we discover ourselves to be, we can try to live as fully as we can within our limitations. In trying, however haltingly, to live positively in this way we are casting our vote in favour of life. The conversion process of beginning to believe in myself, the person God has given me to become, is beginning to take shape in me.

God wants us to be as fully human as we can. There is no other way any of us can be fully human except within our own personal and unique limitations. Some women theologians these days are helping us become more conscious that our limitations are actually our opportunities, providing the raw material with which, in God's providence, each of us has to work. This even implies that the precise way I am a 'victim of sin' will affect the way in which I grow into being more human. For instance, it should give me a sensitivity and compassion for those who are victims of sin in a similar way to myself and it should also make me appreciate the suffering caused by the inhumanity of sin in this particular dimension of human living.

Dorothy Sölle has made the comment: 'I have noticed that people with faith all walk round with a limp'! In other words, each of us will bear our own unique scars of our healed woundedness. Like the glorious wounds of Jesus they will enhance our individual humanity. There is a kind of paradox at play here: the very experience of my woundedness and the inhumanity it brings into my life and that of others is the very stuff out of which repentance and healing are fashioned. It is a classic example of 'felix culpa'. To experience my need for healing and forgiveness is an inescapable stage in the process of being healed and forgiven. Jesus said he did not come to call the just but sinners, and insisted that it was the sick, not the healthy, who need a doctor. If we are to believe in a Saviour, we need to experience our own need of salvation.

(4) The social and ecological implications of a spirituality of growth out of sin

I noted earlier how Aquinas makes the thought-provoking comment: 'God is not offended by us except in so far as we harm ourselves and others.'[9] Not surprisingly, a similar understanding of sin is found centuries later in his fellow Dominican, Albert Nolan, who writes: 'Sin is an offence against God precisely because it is an offence against people. . .There is no such thing as a sin that does not do any harm to anyone. . .In the last analysis sin is not a transgression of law but a transgression of love.'[10]

This approach to sin leads Nolan to make a statement which is at the heart of his whole presentation: 'Sin becomes visible in suffering.'[11] After repeating this statement a few pages further on, he writes: 'If one were to try to discern the new starting point for modern theology and spirituality in most of the Christian world today, one would have to say that it is suffering. The sufferings of so many millions of people on this planet are one of the most fundamental signs of our times.'[12] In other words, Nolan is saying that if we want to know where to find sin in today's world, we need to look at where suffering is to be found. Although he is speaking of suffering brought about by human agency, he is not excluding suffering caused by structural or institutional factors or even, in some cases, suffering caused by so-called accidents and natural disasters. Very often such tragedies have a strong ingredient of human agency in them.

In exploring where God is to be met in today's world Nolan concludes that the voice of God can be heard in the suffering of the oppressed. Their suffering reveals where the need for salvation is most evident in today's world. Following through all the causal links to the very roots of their suffering shows us where conversion is called for. This conversion will bring with it salvation through a changing of the oppressive relationships causing these sufferings. Radical conversion alone suffices and that entails a disowning of the oppressive system and appropriate participation in the processes needed to dismantle it.

Applying this more specifically to the apartheid situation in South Africa in 1988 (the era in which his book was published), Nolan writes: '. . . unless we, both white and black, face the monstrous reality of evil and suffering in South Africa, we shall not find God and we shall not hear his good news of salvation from sin.'[13]

P. T. McCormick, in his article 'Human Sinfulness: Models for a Developing Moral Theology',[14] writes in a similar mode to Nolan when he explores the notion of 'co-operative' or 'social' sin. Recognising that we are interdependent social beings, McCormick argues that we need to develop 'an anthropology which transcends the limits of individualism and incorporates the insights of a growing body of evidence about the social character of the human person.'[15] He goes on to suggest what this anthropology might look like:

> Such an anthropology needs to recognize that experience and reality are transpersonal, reaching beyond both individualism and a localized interpersonality. There must also be a recognition of the essential intersubjectivity or communitarian character of human personhood, a character neither extrinsic nor secondary to the experience of being a person. This means that human freedom is radically interpersonal in its experience and expression. Personal freedom is contextualized and actualized within the organism of the interpersonal human community.[16]

Some structures which are found in the social dimension of human life can with justification be labelled 'sinful' – and this for two reasons. First of all, they are *person-injuring*. They destroy relationships based on justice and freedom and replace them by 'oppressive political and economic systems, developing pervasive social attitudes or voices of greed, hostility, indifference and narcissism.'[17] The result is what McCormick calls 'anti-communities antithetical to the Kingdom of God'. Secondly, these structures do not exist outside of human persons willing to accept and maintain them and working cooperatively within them. It is the actual cooperative effort of the individual members of the group or society which makes up the structure itself. As McCormick writes: 'Cooperation may take a number of forms and the degree of participation or responsibility may differ widely from member to member. However, systemic injustice and oppression depend upon a broad base of diverse sorts of cooperative effort.'[18] Moreover, part of their *person-injuring* character lies in the fact that they can even affect a person's 'core experiences of freedom and dignity'. Consequently, these sinful structures can be self-generating to the extent that people allow themselves to be conditioned into accepting them as either normal or at least inevitable and unavoidable. 'That's life', as the fatalistic saying goes. McCormick puts this point well:

> Members ... respond to their weakened and contextualized freedom with learned patterns of behaviour which support the ongoing relationships of injustice and/or contribute to the progressive disintegration of the group. Such cycles are ongoing, incorporating new members and generations in structures of oppressive and alienating injustice.[19]

It could even be argued that social sin is the prime analogue of sin. If this is true, then the communal celebration of the sacrament of reconciliation should be seen as the most fundamental form of the sacrament because it most clearly expresses this social nature of sin and our co-responsibility for it. The liturgical directive that the fully communal Rite 3 can only be used in an emergency when there is a shortage of confessors completely misses the point of communal celebration. Because sin is primarily communal, our owning or confession of sin should normally be communal, and likewise we should recognise that it needs co-operative effort to undo or heal the harmful consequences of our sin. Such communal commitment to the forgiveness of reality is a prerequisite for our forgiveness. So our hope for and belief in forgiveness also needs to be signified and accepted communally rather than individually.

McCormick would go even further and suggest that clinging on to an individualist interpretation of sin itself constitutes a form of 'social sinfulness' and can be compared to the corporate blindness that Jesus challenged in the Pharisees.[20] Moreover, an individualist interpretation of sin can even be used by groups to 'blind themselves from a sense of sin and responsibility for the structures of injustice which they support.'[21] Social sin, on the other hand, 'instead of positing the origin of evil in anonymous and impersonal structures, reveals how groups of persons co-operate in projecting their responsibility for and participation in systems of injustice on to such invisible and anonymous structures of violence and oppression.'[22]

Jon Sobrino lays great stress on what he calls 'forgiveness of sinful reality'.[23] By this he means the eradication of the structures of oppression and violence and the building of new structures of justice.[24] He even puts this forgiveness of reality before forgiveness of the sinner, though he should not be accused of thinking that a change of structures alone can 'forgive reality'. As he puts it: 'the forgiveness of reality is also a matter of spirituality . . . Forgiving reality means loving, loving very much.'[25]

Finally, creation theology has been slowly bringing home to the Church that there is another dimension of sin that we need to grow out of. This is sometimes called ecological sin. In fact, it opens our eyes to the disturbing truth that there is an ecological dimension in all sin. Humanity is bound up in an intrinsic and essential relationship of interdependence with the rest of creation. There are not two separate and independent ethical criteria operating in ecological issues – what is good for humanity and what is good for creation as a whole. To consider creation as a whole is to consider it as including humanity. It is to recognise humanity as creation reaching a higher level of existence, the level of personal and social consciousness. This level of existence does not constitute a breaking away from the rest of creation. Creational health remains an integral element of the good of humanity, just as does bodily health. And vice versa. In other words, the health of the rest of creation is now dependent on humanity conducting itself in a way which befits its place and responsibility within the whole of creation. Humanity can be a cancerous growth within creation – and some 'deep ecologists' believe it is such already. Or it can be creation reaching out to a yet higher level of life in which it can articulate its hymn of praise and thanksgiving to its creator and reflect in its very way of living the deeply personal and holistic life of its creator. For humanity to distance itself from the rest of creation and lord it over it would be a form of alienation from an integral part of ourselves. At the moment, I believe that we are struggling to find the right language in which to articulate this ecological dimension of sin. It does not seem adequate to say that humanity is nothing more than one part among many within creation, even *primus inter pares*. Yet to say that is not to deny the fact that most of our ethical discourse tends to be too exclusively anthropocentric. It fails to do justice to the oneness of the whole of creation which is being revealed to us through the most recent discoveries in a whole range of scientific disciplines.

Conclusion

The words of Jesus, 'I have come to call not the just but sinners' go hand in hand with his other words, 'I have come that you might have life, and have it more abundantly'.[26] The title of this chapter is 'Saints or sinners? Towards a spirituality of growth out of sin'. I hope that what I have written above has been faithful to the Christian belief that we are both saints and sinners and that a Christian spirituality needs to do justice to both these dimensions. I have tried to show that the notion of 'growth out of sin' can be very helpful at a pastoral level.

Today people are fond of quoting the words of St Irenaeus, 'The glory of God is the human person fully alive'. Perhaps, that truth might be even better expressed through the language of growth, 'The glory of God is the human person becoming more fully alive'. A similar adaptation might even be made to the traditional phrase 'everlasting life'. A spirituality of growth might prefer to speak of 'becoming everlastingly more alive'.

PART 4

Some Pastoral Issues of Life and Death

12

Embryo Research and the Dignity of the Human Person

Introduction

The issues of embryo research might seem far removed from the kind of moral and pastoral issues which are the bread and butter of parish ministry. However, most people at parish level have strong views on abortion, for instance, and wide coverage on TV or in the papers has made them aware of the many new developments in reproductive medicine. Reports about some of the more complicated permutations of in-vitro fertilisation are often in the news and whether they are ethical or not is frequently debated. Many people feel concerned about what is happening. Some are deeply disturbed. Part of developing an adult conscience involves appreciating the complexity of some of these issues and being able to discern what aspects are of greatest significance from a moral or pastoral point of view. In other words, we have to decide what dimensions of this new development need to be considered in our judging whether or not it is in conformity with the Vatican II criterion of the good of the human person 'integrally and adequately considered'.

Embryo research can serve as a useful case study in how to inform our consciences so that we can make a considered moral judgement on such an issue. The public debate over embryo

---

Apart from the Introduction, this chapter originally appeared in *The Month*, February 1990, 59–64, under the title 'Embryo Research: the ethical issues'.

research reminds us that we live in an age of pluralism. Most people we know probably share our basic moral beliefs but many may differ from us in how these beliefs apply to practical everyday life. Where honest and conscientious citizens disagree on practical moral issues, it would be offensive to the dignity of human persons for us to expect our politicians to impose our ethical view on other people of integrity who cannot in conscience accept it.

It might help the reader if I explain the context of the text which follows. On Wednesday 6 December 1989, the Institute of Medical Ethics held a briefing on the issue of embryo research which was open to any Members of both Houses of Parliament who wished to attend. The meeting took place in one of the committee rooms at Westminster and was attended by about six MPs. It took the form of three formal presentations by a panel consisting of Professor Mary Sellers, Professor Robert Edwards and myself. The purpose behind the session was to 'brief' members on the relevant scientific and ethical aspects of the debate. My role was to explain and inform rather than persuade. It was to help them consider all the issues of ethical importance in the important legislative judgement they were asked to make. Because my talk belongs to this particular context, I have decided to leave the text as it stands.

I. Some clarifications

I would like to begin by making one fundamental assumption, a starting point on which I trust we would all agree. It is that our society is founded on respect for the dignity of the human person.

First of all, I would like to comment on three expressions which are often used in ethical discussion on embryo research. I believe these expressions tend to cloud rather than clarify the issue.

'You are playing God'

This expression is often used as an objection against some new application of modern technology to health care or reproductive medicine. As a Christian theologian I believe that humankind is called to exercise responsible stewardship for our world, for ourselves and for future generations. This is a God-given responsibility. In a sense it is an invitation to 'play God'. It is an insult to God to use the phrase 'playing God' to mean taking decisions that are likely to harm or even destroy ourselves and our world. That is not playing God; it is plain stupid. 'Playing God' is accepting our responsibility to do all we can to safeguard and promote the good of our world, humankind and the whole of creation; and that also includes making the best use of human technology. If embryo research could be shown to be 'playing God' in that sense, it would be thoroughly good from an ethical point of view.

'Moral absolute'

This tends to be used in a pejorative sense, based on the presumption that moral absolutes are out. Unfortunately, moral teachers, especially in the Churches, have a habit of proclaiming as an absolute rule what in reality is no more than one factor among many that need to be considered when a moral judgement is being made. This gives 'absolutes' a bad name. Nevertheless, I do not believe that we can exist as a civilised society without believing in at least some absolute values. And foundational among these values is the dignity of the human person. Nuremberg did not simply say: what the Nazis did was evil in those particular circumstances. It denounced what they did as a crime against humanity – now and for ever.

'Slippery slope'

This line of moral argument is often used to claim that once a particular clear demarcation line has been crossed, it becomes impossible to draw the line at any other point and the way lies open to increasingly inhuman behaviour. In itself 'slippery slope' argumentation is not conclusive. Yet it is a helpful challenge to us to check out where the logic of our ethical position is leading us. If it necessarily involves us in accepting things which we know in our heart of hearts are wrong and inhuman, then we know we have gone wrong somewhere. Nevertheless, in itself the question 'where do you draw the line?' should be asking just that – where do you draw the line? To be able to give a satisfactory answer, 'You draw the line here, at this point', can be a major breakthrough in our ethical understanding of a particular problem.

What should we expect from moral philosophy/ Christian ethics?

We should not expect a clear answer to all our ethical problems so that we no longer need to think about them ourselves. What we should expect is help regarding how to think about our problems. Yet even that can be overstated. After all, ethical thinking is not the invention of moral philosophers. Ethical thinking is something basic to human beings. It is one of the major features in our distinctiveness from the rest of creation. I do not know what birds talk about when they chatter together, but it is certainly not about good and evil! Philosophers can help us to be clear-minded and logical in talking about good and evil, but they cannot tell us precisely what is good or evil. That is not a judgement reserved to experts. It is a shared responsibility of the whole human family. Nor is it an easy judgement, especially when it gets down to particular issues. It requires moral sensitivity, experience, an appreciation of tradition which is both reverent and critical, accurate scientific/ factual knowledge, etc. That is why the element of 'common search', stressed by the Vatican II Pastoral Constitution, *The Church in the Modern World*, n. 16, is so important. Arriving at an ethical evaluation of embryo research is a common task and calls for a sharing of all our riches of knowledge and understanding. I would suggest that what should influence us most in trying to evaluate embryo research is not how persuasively or forcefully someone has argued his or her position. That would only encourage special pleading and pressure groups. Perhaps there might be a place for that in politics but there is no room for it in the process of arriving at ethical judgement. Rather I should judge in favour of the view which corresponds most fully to what I believe in my heart of hearts to be good and true, even though I may find it difficult to put it properly into words. I do not believe that such honest heart-searching will result in everyone agreeing with everyone else. But I do believe that if people are prepared really to listen to their own integrity and share it with others, the final communal judgement will probably bring us as close to the truth as we are likely to get for the present. Part of the evil of demanding obedience to external authoritative moral teaching is that it short-circuits this process and makes it more difficult to tap what, in Catholic parlance, is called the 'sensus fidelium'.

Research

There is research and research. There is no ethical problem when research is done for the benefit of the one being experimented on – or at least if it is done in the knowledge that it will not harm him or her and provided that informed consent has been given. Although there is some discussion on the issue of proxy consent, there would likewise be no problem if this was the kind of research being considered in the case of the embryo. Research which is deemed unethical on humans is research which will not benefit the subject and which will actually harm or even kill him or her. The strong revulsion in the face of such research is clearly evidenced in the current debate as to whether it is ethical to use the results of this kind of research carried out by the Nazis in concentration camps. This is the form of research referred to in the debate on embryo research. It is research which is not for the good of *this* embryo and which will harm it and either kill it or result in its death.

II. Why the ethics of embryo research is relevant to Parliamentary debate

Why is embryo research a matter of such concern to the people of our countries that it merits a special Bill and a major debate in both Houses of Parliament? Why could it not just be subsumed under existing legislation dealing with the disposal of human tissue and human organs, etc.?

There are two causes for public concern which make embryo research appropriate matter for Parliament. Both are linked to respect for the dignity of the human person.

The first is the possibility that certain kinds of embryo research might be harmful to our children and future generations and so should be carefully regulated by legislation. This touches on the issue of genetic engineering. Although that topic is really outside my brief, I would nevertheless like to offer one or two comments.

A major ethical distinction needs to be drawn between genetic engineering which is 'therapeutic' and that which is 'eugenic'. The first is directed towards setting right defects in genetic make-up; the second moves into the field of quality breeding.

What is even more important is to look carefully at the life-philosophies that can underlie these forms of engineering. The 'therapeutic' variety can stem from that same wholesome concern which motivates our general research into preventative medicine. However, we would need to check lest it might come from a far less wholesome motivation, one which would look on the handicapped as subhuman, a stigma and a threat to a healthy society and a wasteful drain on our scarce resources. Likewise, we would need to be discerning in the case of 'eugenic' engineering. There is nothing unethical about prospective parents having high hopes for the good all-round health and positive giftedness of their children. That is very different from an attitude which puts such high value on potential achievement that acceptance of a child is made conditional on its having the desired qualities. Though attitudes are impossible to legislate for, legislation itself has its own intentionality. Let us hope that the intentionality of any future legislation on genetic engineering will be therapeutic and eugenic only in the wholesome sense noted above.

The second cause for public concern which makes embryo research an appropriate subject for parliamentary debate is the fact that there is a strong body of opinion in our countries that believes that the dignity of the human person is involved when we are dealing with the human embryo.

It is important to notice that this is a very different kind of moral argument from the previous one. The previous one involved a 'weighing up of pros and cons' form of moral argumentation, i.e. weighing up the possible good and bad consequences of embryo research. Such a weighing up of pros and cons is the normal procedure that we use in most of our moral decision-making. However, I feel sure that none of us here would be happy about applying that kind of argumentation to the issue of harmful experimentation on young children – or on adults for that matter. At Nuremberg, and in the subsequent Declaration of Helsinki, we said a firm 'no' to destructive research on human beings. We condemned it as a crime against humanity.

I stress this point because in the discussion about embryo research tremendous claims are made about the benefits that would accrue to humanity from such research. It is not for me to judge how valid these claims are. The point I am making is that even if these claims are one hundred per cent true, they do not constitute a conclusive argument for embryo research. If a convincing case could be made out for saying that the embryo is already a human person, we would be forced to acknowledge that all the positive advantages of embryo research would be ethically irrelevant – just as we would consider possible major benefits from destructive research on our children to be ethically irrelevant.

So this second cause for public concern forces us to examine very carefully the issue of the status of the human embryo.

III. The main issues in the debate on the status of the human embryo

A. *What we would all agree on*

I suggest that there are a number of points about which we would all agree.

1. What makes human beings special, and so different from all other species on our planet, might be fairly generally described as our capacity for self-awareness, reasoning, moral evaluation, freedom and responsibility.
2. Underlying these fundamental human properties we recognise the essential prerequisite of individuality. There must be an individual subject in whom these properties reside. 'Self'-awareness is not a collective activity. It presupposes a 'self' who is aware. We refer to such an individual human subject as a human person.

3. We do not deny personhood to someone who has never had or who has lost these fundamental human capacities e.g. someone who is severely mentally handicapped or senile. We describe such a one as a handicapped person, not as a non-person.
4. Likewise, we do not deny personhood to a human being who has not yet reached the stage of proper awareness e.g. a baby. We do not believe that a baby lacks human dignity and so can be killed. I am aware that a few philosophers do deny personhood to the handicapped, the senile and babies and would argue that there is no intrinsic moral objection to killing them. I am assuming that most MPs – and their constituents – would find that position morally repugnant and a contradiction to the basic values we all believe in. Deep down we recognise that babies, the mentally handicapped and the senile are *fellow human beings*, even though they may not have the *actual* capacity for self-awareness, rationality etc.

B. Some implications of what we agree on

Our recognition of the human dignity of a baby implies that we are prepared to recognise human personhood in an individual human being who does not yet have actual capacity for self-awareness etc. We sometimes express that by saying that a baby has the 'potential' for self-awareness etc., but that this potential cannot yet be activated.

If we are prepared to say that about this tiny baby, this bundle of potential, we are forced to face the question: what then about the foetus, or the embryo? They too are bundles of potential. Should we recognise human dignity in them too?

This brings us into the heart of the most difficult ethical question raised by embryo research. Some people dismiss it as unanswerable, but that is to opt out of serious moral debate. Admittedly, it is an extremely difficult question requiring careful philosophical thinking. And it does not yield the same kind of certainty that is found in empirical scientific research. Yet that does not mean that we cannot hope for that quality of certainty which is sufficient to justify our human decision-making in most other important areas of human life. It is not a mere coincidence that we refer to this certainty as *moral* certainty.

C. How can we tell we are dealing with a person?

None of us would claim that an ovum or a sperm are persons, even though they are forms of human life. Neither would we deny that a baby is a person. Between those two clear extremes there lies the whole long process of inter-uterine human development. Embryologists inform us that the life process is continuous from generation to generation. There is no point in the human developmental process at which it can be said, 'Human life begins here'. Consequently, many embryologists involved in the embryo research debate claim that any cut-off point for research is bound to be arbitrary. That may be true embryologically but it is not necessarily true philosophically. The philosophical question is not 'When did human life begin?' but 'When did I begin?', as Norman Ford expresses it so succinctly in the title of his book referred to below.

What I propose to do is to look at three different criteria for personhood which are put forward by philosophers. There are other views besides these three but these seem to represent most of the philosophical writing I have come across on this question. Moreover, they are all capable of 'realist' interpretation. What I mean by realism in this connection is the acknowledgement that human dignity is not something we confer on others by some kind of social contract. It is something intrinsic which we recognise and respect. In that sense all three of these positions are reconcilable with a Christian theology of creation in which we recognise all human persons as 'gift' from God and beings of transcendental dignity and not merely of functional worth.

First View: INDIVIDUALITY - as soon as you have an individual human being, you have a being endowed with the full dignity of human personhood

Among those who hold this view there is some disagreement as to when individuation occurs. Some hold it is at fertilisation; others hold that definitive individuation only occurs with the emergence of the primitive streak (around fourteen days).

The 'fertilization' view is the position taught by the Roman Catholic Church. Although there is no reason to suggest that those who hold this view are not convinced of its truth, the official Roman Catholic statement of this position also includes a kind of 'safety first' gloss. In other words, it asserts that this position cannot be disproved and so human prudence demands that this view should be followed; otherwise, one would risk killing a human being, and running such a risk would in itself be immoral. The principal thrust of this line of argument is that fertilisation is the key moment, since it is at this point that a unique genetic blueprint is laid down and there is continuity of development from this stage onwards. In a 1980 joint statement, the Roman Catholic Archbishops of Great Britain insisted that an individual's personal history begins at this point. This view is very far from being the exclusive preserve of Roman Catholics. I have recently had occasion to read for review six books dealing with embryo research and related topics. Three of them argued the 'fertilisation' position very forcefully and all three were by writers in the Protestant tradition. In the two books by Roman Catholic writers, the 'fertilisation' position was viewed very critically.

The 'primitive streak' view is held by many today, including a number of prominent Roman Catholic moral theologians. For instance, this position is argued very painstakingly by the Australian Roman Catholic philosopher and moral theologian, Norman Ford, in his carefully researched book, *When did I begin? Conception of the Human Individual in History, Philosophy and Science.*[1] It is interesting to note that Mary Warnock, in her Foreword to Ford's book, expresses her agreement with his position and maintains that from this stage we are dealing with a 'human individual of infinite worth'. This view shares the basic 'individuality' stance of the 'fertilisation' position. However, it cannot accept that fertilisation is the marker event for individuality. Its reading of recent embryological evidence indicates that individuation is not definitive until the formation of the primitive streak. Ford writes: 'Instead of viewing development in the first two weeks after fertilisation as development of the human individual, I have argued the process ought to be seen as one of development into a human individual.' Ford writes as an Aristotelian philosopher, a major school of thought today. A position similar to his has been expressed by Anthony Kenny, former Master of Balliol and a leading English philosopher.

Presumably those who hold the 'primitive streak' version of the 'individuality' position could not oppose embryo research on the grounds that it violates the dignity of a human person. Hence, any other disvalues they see in it would be evaluated by the 'weighing up of pros and cons' form of moral reasoning. Obviously, those who hold the 'fertilisation' version will be opposed to embryo research at any time. In fact, Pope John Paul II has condemned it 'in the most formal and explicit way', and it has been likewise condemned by the 1987 Instruction, *Donum Vitae*, of the Congregation for the Doctrine and the Faith. It has been strongly opposed too by Oliver O'Donovan, Professor of Christian Ethics at Oxford and a leading Anglican ethicist.

Second View: Rudimentary organic structure prerequisite for self-awareness etc.

This view is followed by other Aristotelian philosophers. In fact, its precedent can be found in Aristotle himself – and in Aquinas following him – and in much of the history of the Roman Catholic Church, influenced by both. In other words, to express Aristotle's view somewhat over-simply, a human soul can only be the life form of an organism which is human in a substantial way. Obviously, no one today would accept the biology of Aristotle or Aquinas. Nevertheless, many philosophers and theologians still accept their basic premise about the need for a biological grounding of true personhood. In fact, this premise is not peculiar to this view. It is shared by those who hold the first view and the dispute between its two versions actually hinges on whether a specific genetic blueprint constitutes a sufficient biological grounding for personhood.

Holders of this second view appeal partially to the evidence from evolution, which seems to point to a kind of developmental hominisation. They would see a somewhat similar process at work in the developing embryo/foetus. There are hints of that in the position put forward very tentatively by Professor Jack Mahoney in his book, *Bioethics and Belief*.[2]

Nevertheless, although recognising the unbroken continuity of the biological developmental process, this view would not be arguing for a kind of developing personhood. It would want to focus on 'some recognizably early point in embryonic development' and would acknowledge personhood from that point onwards. As regards when that point might be, Peter Byrne, in arguing the modern Aristotelian case for this position, writes: 'embryos may properly be treated as less than persons up to the point where brain and nervous system come to be laid down as differentiated types of tissues' – and he goes on to suggest a cut-off date of two months after fertilisation.[3]

Those who hold this view would probably allow embryo research during the period prior to such rudimentary organic structure being formed, provided, of course, it could be justified according to normal 'weighing of pros and cons' argumentation.

Third View: Rudimentary subjective experience - a person is essentially a 'subject' and so development has not yet reached the personal stage until there is some rudimentary subjective experience

This is essentially different from a utilitarian position which might allow embryo research provided no pain was caused. Modern anaesthesia makes the avoidance of pain relatively easy. However, 'cause no pain' offers no kind of moral criterion for judging when we are faced with a human person.

The subjective experience criterion is quite different from that. It argues that there is no person if there is no human subject. And there is no human subject prior to some initial and rudimentary form of subjective experience. One recent writer, Carol Tauer, arguing this position, suggests that the capacity to retain experience, even at an unconscious level, constitutes the most elementary form of human experience.[3] Although unconscious, this experience has continuity with the experience of a fully developed person and is already determining the psychological development of the individual. Hence, she speaks of the psychic basis for personhood. She would locate the beginnings of such experience at the time of earliest brainstem activity, i.e. during the seventh week of development. Once again, prior to this, this position would presumably have no moral objection to embryo research, provided it was not excluded for other reasons on the basis of the weighing of pros and cons.

D. Creating embryos specifically for research

If embryos are considered not to be human persons, does that mean that they have no moral significance and are just like any other piece of isolated human tissue?

Some people who are prepared to accept embryo research in principle want it to be restricted to spare embryos (i.e. those obtained in the IVF process but found to be surplus to needs or unsuitable for interuterine development). They are opposed to 'creating' embryos specifically for embryo research. This question was discussed by the Warnock Commission[4] and four members even went so far as to write an 'expression of dissent' which is included as Appendix C in the Report. The same question also came up for discussion in the 1986 CIBA Symposium. There Professor Gordon Dunstan argues in favour of creating embryos for research, and seems to suggest that such embryos would have a different moral significance because of the specific intention for bringing them into existence. Moreover, he adds a consequentialist argument that in the long run this might reduce the numbers of embryos used for research since researchers would be working with better specimens. I leave you to judge whether you find this a convincing line of argument.

An alternative approach would be to argue that, although such early embryos might not have the intrinsic dignity of a human person, nevertheless they would have some intrinsic moral significance because of what they could develop into, given time and the right environment and external stimuli. I suspect that this is what Professor Mahoney is referring to when he speaks of the 'intrinsic promise' of such embryos. How we treat them has a bearing on our sense of reverence for our own humanity. I must admit that, even if one accepts such a line of argument (or one on somewhat similar lines), it is hardly a conclusive argument against either embryo research in general or the creation of embryos specifically for research. Nevertheless, it does acknowledge that we are working in an area of profound moral significance and hence we should try to formulate prudent criteria governing our activity here.

Conclusion

I have not tried to argue one particular position. I have tried to be faithful to my task of providing a briefing on the kind of issues that lie at the heart of any ethical consideration of embryo research.

I am not an agnostic who believes that the truth is impossible to arrive at. Nor am I a relativist who believes that the truth is simply what each of us makes of it. I hope I am a realist who believes that the truth is something we can and must strive for – and who hopes that we can achieve it, at least partially. To my mind, the divergence of views on embryo research is an indication that together we have not yet arrived at a completely satisfactory grasp and articulation of the truth relevant to this particular topic. Yet that should not tempt us to give up our quest for the truth and settle for mere expediency. My hope is that the current debate, in society as a whole and in both Houses of Parliament, will be a step forward in our quest for the truth.

Meantime, you face the difficult task of voting on such an divisive issue. I am naive enough to cherish the hope that if every MP were to vote according to his or her honest and carefully considered ethical judgement, the chances are that the result might be a fairly good guide to the truth insofar as we can grasp it at present. However, arriving at an honest and carefully considered ethical judgement is no easy matter. It is certainly not helped by the emotional and other forms of pressure to which MPs are being subjected both by the supporters and the opponents of embryo research. The freedom to be respected in the 'free' vote on this important matter can be violated in other ways besides pressure from party whips.

13

Prolonging Life Unduly or Letting Die: Christian Morality – Pro-life or Pro-person?

In my ministry as a priest in a parish I am often involved with cancer patients and their families struggling with difficult decisions about what treatment will be best for them. Rarely is their overriding concern about which treatment will prolong their life the longest. Almost invariably they are more concerned about how the treatment will affect their lives. They desperately want to stay alive for as long as they can live their lives with dignity, able to appreciate and enjoy the love of their family and friends. But they do not want special medical procedures to be used which will extend their lives beyond that point. To many people their attitude is just common sense. I believe it is also based on a deep Christian faith which sees death in the context of a fuller life to come and which believes that medicine is made for persons and not persons for medicine.

Traditional Roman Catholic medical ethics

This solid, down-to-earth approach is affirmed by traditional Roman Catholic medical ethics. Over the years moral theologians writing in this field have refused to view life as an

---

The issue of prolonging life had also been hotly debated in the public forum. This chapter is made up of a combination of parts of two articles I wrote in 1993 when the Tony Bland case was under discussion: 'A Medical Dilemma', in *The Month*, 1993, 138-44, and 'Rest for Tony Bland', in *The Tablet*, 13 March 1993, 332-5.

absolute value. Consequently, they never taught that we must keep physical life going for as long as possible. For them the goodness of human life is bound up with the fact that it is the life of a human person. Hence, an important factor to be considered in assessing any particular life-sustaining medical procedure is: how alive will it keep me as a human person? Will it enable me to live a relatively normal life or will it leave me seriously incapacitated in some way or other? While they would have no truck with any suggestion that killing, or its equivalent, could be part of medicine, they always refused to accept that a patient is obliged to take every available means to sustain life for as long as possible.

The underlying question which occasioned the development of this teaching was: is a person whose health is affected by a life-threatening condition obliged to undergo whatever medical treatment will prolong life? The answer that eventually came to be given to that question was: it all depends. Normally there is an obligation only if two conditions are fulfilled, namely, (1) the treatment brings real benefit to the patient; and (2) the treatment is not disproportionately burdensome. These two conditions, though distinct, were seen as forming a coherent whole in the decision-making process and safeguarding the important insight that simply staying alive is not the most important thing for human persons. What is at least equally important is the kind of lives we are able to lead.

Among the Roman Catholic moral theologians prior to Vatican II who played a major role in developing this tradition were two U.S. Jesuits whose textbooks became virtually required reading for seminarians, priests and Catholic doctors: Gerald Kelly, *Medico-Moral Problems*[1] and Edwin Healy, *Medical Ethics*.[2]

With regard to the appropriate care of patients with a life-threatening medical condition the position of Kelly and Healy could be summed up roughly under the following points:

1. What is meant by a 'life-threatening condition' embraces far more than the final stages of the dying process, even though, not surprisingly, many of the cases Kelly and Healy discuss come into that latter category. A life-threatening

condition is considered to be present when it is impossible to preserve life without some kind of medical intervention.

2. The fundamental question is whether a patient in such a life-threatening condition is obliged to undergo every medical treatment needed to preserve life. The issue of prolonging the dying process is subsidiary to this main question.
3. For patients in this condition the only treatment that is obligatory is that which is deemed to be 'ordinary'. 'Extraordinary' treatment is optional.
4. Whether treatment is deemed ordinary or extraordinary does not depend simply on whether it is ordinarily available or not. The meaning of ordinary and extraordinary is much more subtle than that. Moreover, it has considerable in-built flexibility since it involves looking at a whole variety of factors. Kelly, for instance, defines as extraordinary 'all medicines, treatments, and operations, which cannot be obtained or used without excessive expense, pain, or other inconvenience, or which, if used, would not offer a reasonable hope of benefit.'[3] Hence, there is no cut-and-dried classified list of ordinary and extraordinary medical procedures. The Congregation for the Doctrine of the Faith offers a helpful clarification when it notes that most recent writers prefer to use the terms 'proportionate' and 'disproportionate' to express the same basic insight (cf. p. 196). That captures much better the point that Kelly and Healy are making.
5. The judgement whether a treatment is obligatory or not is a matter of assessing whether, all things considered, a life-sustaining medical intervention is in line with the best interests of the patient as a human person. The 'all things' to be considered are very wide-ranging. They are not limited to whatever directly affects the patient. They also include other features such as the cost of the treatment, scarcity of resources, the impact on the family, etc.
6. Considering 'all things' is a matter of assessing both the benefits and the burdens resulting from sustaining life by medical intervention. The very fact that the benefits and

burdens of prolonging life are weighed up implies that the mere prolongation of life itself is not an absolute good which cannot be weighed against other goods.

7. Foregoing or even withdrawing a medical procedure which is deemed an extraordinary means of sustaining life is not equivalent to killing. It is merely allowing the dying process to take its course ('letting die') when the only alternative would be some treatment which, in terms of overall benefit and burden, is judged to be humanly undesirable and so not obligatory. Killing, on the other hand, means either actively causing death or withdrawing or omitting some treatment which, all things considered, is an ordinary – and so humanly reasonable and obligatory – means of sustaining life in terms of overall benefit and burden. This distinction between 'killing' and 'letting die', though disputed by some philosophers, enables our writers to draw a clear dividing line between legitimate instances of 'letting die' and those which are ethically the equivalent of euthanasia and which they totally reject.
8. The decision to withdraw or not to use life-prolonging medical procedures is a decision about appropriate care. It is not a decision to give up caring for the patient. Paul Ramsey's short dictum 'Never abandon care' still applies even when the only care that can be given is comfort and company – and that can sometimes be very costly on the carers. If the patient is in pain or discomfort, pain relief and normal nursing care will also be considered appropriate care. What about feeding? In his 1958 doctoral dissertation Daniel A. Cronin, now Archbishop of Hartford, USA, after a review of over fifty moral theologians, from Aquinas to the present day, concluded: 'Even natural means, such as taking of food and drink, can become optional if taking them requires great effort or if the hope of beneficial results is not present.'[4] Consequently, ordinary human feeding is usually part of appropriate care but, in some instances, would not be so when it causes the patient great physical and mental discomfort while providing little or no real benefit. It is sometimes argued that intravenous nutrition

and hydration should never be withdrawn since it would be withdrawing ordinary human care. That is certainly not in line with the tradition of moral theology I have been describing. It is true that Healy recognises that intravenous feeding is a normal procedure for tiding many patients over the immediate post-operative phase of their treatment until they recover. That is why he states that 'as a rule' intravenous feeding should be regarded as an ordinary means. However, I feel certain that Kelly and Healy would never have argued that intravenous nutrition and hydration is obligatory for people in a dying condition who cannot be fed normally on the grounds that it is simply part of ordinary human care for them. Referring to what he calls 'the moderate standard', Gerald Kelly writes:

> I once asked the mother superior of a home for incurable cancer patients whether they used such things as intravenous feeding to prolong life. She replied that they did not. They gave all patients devoted nursing care; they tried to alleviate pain; and they helped the patients to make the best possible spiritual preparation for death. Many very good people with whom I have spoken about this matter think these sisters have the right idea – 'the good Christian attitude toward life and death', as they call it. This is really an exemplification of the moderate standard.[5]

9. When a person is in a life-threatening condition, the length of time by which life can be prolonged is not, in itself, the only relevant factor in deciding whether treatment is ordinary or extraordinary. That is true, even when it seems possible to prolong life over a number of years. In the wide variety of examples Kelly and Healy examine, their underlying principle is always the same. Although life is an important human value, it is not an absolute value. Hence, when it is a matter of judging whether one is obliged to take certain means to preserve one's life, a whole variety of factors can come into the equation, not all of them directly related to the person whose life is threatened.

10. Since the issue concerns whether the good of the patient as a human person will be served by having his life sustained by medical intervention, ideally the patient should make this decision.
11. If the patient through age or infirmity is unable to decide, then the decision belongs to those closest to the patient, husband, wife, parents or guardians. Kelly insists that they do not make the decision 'in their own name, but rather as representing the patient; hence, they should try to determine what he would reasonably want done under the circumstances.'[6] How such a reasonable interpretation of the patient's wishes is to be made is explained very clearly by Kelly when he looks at a situation where the doctor has to take the decision:

> The doctor should follow the plan previously suggested for the relatives: that is, try to make a prudent estimate of what the patient would reasonably want if he could be asked. This would mean that the doctor would do what he sincerely judged to be for the best interests of his patient. If other means are lacking for determining this, the golden rule should be helpful. What would the doctor himself want if he were in the patient's condition?[7]

I think two other points could be added to this list. They are not explicitly stated by our writers but would seem to follow from the general position they have developed. These two points are not without importance for the contemporary debate about foregoing medically-assisted feeding for patients in a persistent vegetative state (PVS).

12. Although 'quality of life' is not an expression normally used by Kelly and Healy, they would have recognised the important consideration to which it is referring. In looking at life-sustaining means they certainly believed that account should be taken of the sort of life it would enable a person to live. Healy, for instance, takes considerations of this kind into account when he looks at the case of a

patient faced with a leg amputation. He attaches important ethical significance to how a patient views the kind of life this medical intervention will enable him to live. Healy accepts that, other things being equal, the amputation may be judged to be non-obligatory because of the 'hardship and shame' a patient might experience in living his life with the disability of a prosthetic leg.[8]

13. Kelly would even argue that a patient can have a legitimate desire to die. In discussing the view of J. J. McCarthy[9] that 'a patient may not discontinue the use of extraordinary means with the intention of shortening life as the immediate object of the act', he comments: 'Would all moralists agree with this? Since extraordinary means are not obligatory for the patient, and since the desire for death can be licit, I do not see why extraordinary means may not be omitted precisely because of a legitimate desire for death.'[10] In a footnote he mentions Palmieri's opinion (similar to Healy above) that 'the dread of living with a mutilated body might excuse one from undergoing an amputation.' I presume Kelly is implicitly saying that if a person is being kept alive by medical means in a state of severe pain or major incapacity, it would be legitimate for him to ask to be allowed to die by foregoing this treatment rather than to be made to continue living in such a state.

Official Roman Catholic teaching

The medical ethics tradition developed by these moral theologians found acceptance in the Church at large and was strongly affirmed by Pius XII in a statement made in 1957:

> Normally one is held to use only ordinary means – according to circumstances of persons, places, times and culture – that is to say, means that do not involve any grave burden for oneself or another. A more strict obligation would be too burdensome for most people and would render the attainment of the higher, more important good too difficult. Life, health, all temporal activities are in fact subordinated to spiritual ends.[11]

In more recent years this same tradition has been reiterated by the Congregation for the Doctrine of the Faith in its 1980 *Declaration on Euthanasia*. Aware of the danger that modern technology can be used in a way which is abusive to the dying person, the CDF Declaration is content to go along with the expression 'right to die', provided it does not imply a right to 'procure death either by one's own hand or by means of someone else' but simply means 'the right to die peacefully with human and Christian dignity'. It stresses that any decision regarding treatment pertains ultimately 'to the conscience either of the sick person, or of those qualified to speak in the sick person's name, or of the doctors to decide in the light of moral obligations and of the various aspects of the case.'

As mentioned above, the CDF Declaration notes that many writers today prefer the terms proportionate and disproportionate to ordinary and extraordinary. This does not alter the traditional teaching, which it strongly upholds, that normally a patient is not obliged to undergo extraordinary treatment to sustain life. The factors it suggests for consideration in assessing the use of any kind of treatment include 'its degree of complexity or risk, its cost and possibilities of using it' and also 'the result that can be expected, taking into account the state of the sick person and his or her physical and moral resources.' When life-sustaining treatment is already in use and a decision has to be made whether to continue it or not, it suggests that

> account will have to be taken of the reasonable wishes of the patient's family, as also of the advice of the doctors who are specially competent in the matter. The latter may in particular judge that the investment in instruments and personnel is disproportionate to the results foreseen; they may also judge that the techniques applied impose on the patient strain or suffering out of proportion with the benefits which he or she may gain from such techniques.

It insists that 'such a refusal is not the equivalent of suicide; on the contrary, it should be considered as an acceptance of the human condition, or a wish to avoid the application of a medical procedure disproportionate to the results that can be expected, or a desire not to impose excessive expense on the family or the community.'

The Catechism of the Catholic Church, published in 1994,[12] also upholds this tradition. After a clear rejection of direct euthanasia, it continues:

> Discontinuing medical procedures that are burdensome, dangerous, extraordinary, or disproportionate to the expected outcome can be legitimate; it is the refusal of 'over-zealous' treatment. Here one does not will to cause death; one's inability to impede it is merely accepted. The decision should be made by the patient if he is competent and able or, if not, by those legally entitled to act for the patient, whose reasonable will and legitimate interests must always be respected.
>
> Even if death is thought imminent, the ordinary care owed to a sick person cannot be legitimately interrupted. The use of painkillers to alleviate the sufferings of the dying, even at the risk of shortening their days, can be morally in conformity with human dignity if death is not willed as either an end or a means but only foreseen and tolerated as inevitable. (nn. 2278-9)

The persistent vegetative state (PVS)

The persistent vegetative state and the ethical dilemmas associated with it have come on the scene since the time of Kelly and Healy. What would have been their position regarding the withdrawal of medical feeding and hydration from a PVS patient? One can only make an informed guess in the light of their general Christian approach to matters of life and death and their basic understanding of the purpose and limits of good medicine.

I have no doubt that these writers would have strongly defended the moral legitimacy of a decision to withdraw medical nutrition and hydration when a PVS diagnosis indicates, as reliably as is humanly possible at the present time, that there is no foreseeable prospect of any improvement in the patient's condition. That is not to deny the difficulties involved in such a diagnosis, as a few recent cases have revealed.

Our writers would not have seen withdrawal of medical nutrition and hydration in such a case as being an instance of killing. For them it would have been a legitimate instance of 'letting die'. Moreover, for them the fact that a PVS patient can be kept alive by medical feeding and hydration for many years would be beside the point. They would have said that what is relevant is not whether the patient is at this moment in time in the actual process of dying but whether his or her condition is life-threatening in the sense that, without continued medical intervention, life would not be able to be sustained. I believe they would have fully agreed with writers today who say that the persistent vegetative state constitutes a fatal pathology for the patient. In fact, a fatal pathology is simply another expression for what they meant by a life-threatening condition. They would have endorsed the analysis offered by Kevin O'Rourke:

> By definition, a patient in an irreversible coma cannot eat and swallow and thus will die of that pathology in a short time unless life-prolonging devices are utilized to circumvent the pathology. Withholding artificial hydration and nutrition from a patient in an irreversible coma does not induce a new fatal pathology; rather, it allows an already existing fatal pathology to take its natural course. Hence, when making ethical or legal decisions concerning the care of persons in an irreversible coma or with other serious pathological conditions, rather than discussing whether death is imminent or whether a patient is terminally ill, we should ask whether a fatal pathology is present.[13]

They would also have approved the Texan bishops' use of the same analysis and their final conclusion drawn from it: 'The morally appropriate foregoing or withdrawing of artificial nutrition and hydration from a permanently unconscious person is not abandoning that person. Rather, it is accepting the fact that the person has come to the end of his or her pilgrimage and should not be impeded from taking the final step.'[14]

For Healy and Kelly both the treatment itself and the kind of life it sustained were relevant factors in the patient's judgement. If they had been consulted in the case of Tony Bland, for instance, I feel sure that they would have strongly defended the legitimacy of the decision taken by Tony's parents and his doctor. I suspect they would have considered the outside offers to keep him alive and care for him as, to say the least, insensitive and misguided, however well intentioned. Implicit in these offers seemed to be the assumption that the decision to forego further treatment was not a caring decision. I believe that our writers, recognising the very devoted care of Tony's parents, doctor and nursing staff, would have interpreted the decision to forego further medical feeding as being a decision about the most appropriate way of caring for Tony, rather than as a denial of care. And they would have respected that decision, knowing it must have been taken only after great heart-searching and anguish. I feel sure they would have been in complete agreement with the observations of Dr Sheila Cassidy, writing out of her long experience as a medical practitioner in hospice care:

> It is important for the lay person to understand the difference, as medical people see it, between ordinary and 'extraordinary' means of treatment. If a person is unable to eat or drink because his brain is damaged, then he will die. He will die of the primary disease, which has rendered him incapable of taking nourishment. Now when someone has a stroke or a head injury, we have no immediate means of knowing whether or not he has the potential to recover – whether the brain disease is reversible. Such patients are therefore kept alive by *extraordinary* means, by intravenous infusions or tubes down their noses and into their stomachs. They must be turned every two hours if they are not to get terrible bed sores and their bowels are cleared by digital removal of faeces from the rectum. All this is very intensive and invasive nursing. It is life-saving in those patients whose brain damage is transitory. But it is not an *ordinary* way to nurse people and it is not appropriate to continue it indefinitely in those patients with irreversible brain damage.
>
> I do not believe, therefore, that the decision to stop Tony Bland's extraordinary care is a step along the path to euthanasia. Like Fr Kevin Kelly in his recent *Tablet* article I believe it is an intelligent, humane and Christian way to

> treat a person whose body has been so badly damaged that it can no longer sustain life. I do not for one moment think that such legislation will lead to the quiet extermination of old ladies with Alzheimer's disease or the congenitally handicapped. By the grace of God (and it really is the grace of God) there are nurses who feel called to do the ordinary caring tasks for the elderly and the profoundly handicapped. They willingly wash and feed and love the feeble of brain, spooning custard patiently into aimless mouths and talking lovingly to those who never answer. Such care is right and proper – for it is *ordinary* caring and involves no tubes, no respirators and no high-tech medicine.[15]

Healy and Kelly would have insisted, of course, that their making such a judgement in no way calls into question the intrinsic human dignity of the patient or his or her innate right to appropriate treatment and care. In fact, for them the importance of considering such factors actually flows from the patient's dignity as a human person and his or her right to exercise legitimate freedom and responsibility in deciding what health-care is appropriate. Moreover, they would have strongly denied that their view poses any threat to the elderly or to people suffering from severe mental illness. The condition of such people is not medically life threatening and hence is not affected by this discussion.

In some Catholic discussions of the withdrawal of medical nutrition and hydration from a PVS patient the main insight of our Roman Catholic medical ethics tradition seems to be in danger of being lost. One gets the impression that the human good of being alive is regarded as a quasi-absolute value. That is departing from the pro-person emphasis of the tradition and moving to a depersonalised pro-life position. I suspect that Kelly and Healy would be much more in sympathy with the view of Shannon and Walter when they remind us that 'while preserving life is a good – and even a great good – biological life is neither the highest value nor a value that holds ultimate claim on us. To make biological life the ultimate value is to forget our real priorities and to create an idol by making a lesser good our ultimate reality.'[16]

Kelly favours what he describes as a 'moderate attitude' in caring for patients in a life-threatening condition. He cautions against a more extreme attitude which can occasion

> great nervous strain for relatives when they are forced to watch day after day at the bedside of an unconscious father, mother, brother, etc., whose thread of life is being kept intact by intravenous feeding, oxygen, and such things. The moderate attitude is less likely to impose such burdens...There are limits to what must or should be done in order to prolong temporal life. This is what I mean by the 'good Catholic' attitude.[17]

All this seems good sound Christian common sense. It is the same kind of attitude I find in the people in my parish. Richard McCormick has obviously tapped into a similar experience: 'The vast majority of people with whom I have discussed this question agree without hesitation that it is humanly "useless" and "futile" to provide nutrition-hydration to those in a persistent vegetative state.' In fact, he even goes so far as to write: 'Those who would count mere vegetative life a patient-benefit have, I believe, slipped their grasp on the heart of Catholic tradition in this matter.'[18] A decision that the human cost involved in sustaining life by a particular medical intervention is disproportionate to any resulting benefit is not rooted in the selfish individualism of radical autonomy and self-determination which can so easily lead to an acceptance of euthanasia. Rather it is set firmly in the belief of our medical ethics tradition that life, though intrinsically valuable, is not an absolute value. Sometimes the cost of sustaining it by medical intervention is too high in terms of the patient's own human dignity and that of his family and those caring for him. The Jesuit moral theologian, John Paris, repeats McCormick's warning about letting slip one's grasp on the heart of Catholic tradition and goes on to say: 'It is that tradition, developed over centuries of living out the Gospel message on the meaning of life and death ... that is and ought to be the source of the Catholic Church's teaching on the use of nutrition and fluids.'[19]

Another writer even suggests that it is precisely our medical technology which has made the persistent vegetative state possible: 'In deliberately prescribing treatments that prolong the lives of patients in a vegetative state, we are causing the persistent vegetative state.'[20] Shannon and Walter put the same point slightly differently when they note that the burden in the case of PVS patients is 'iatrogenic'. In other words, it is modern medical technology which has created this burdensome condition. They go on to say: 'Although it is doubtful that the PVS patient would experience this burden personally, the burden is real, even if experienced secondhand by the family and/or by those professionals who must care for the patient.'[21] This is an honest recognition that medicine can sometimes lose touch with its basic beneficial purpose and end up by burdening persons and their loved ones. As Shannon and Walter put it: 'While foregoing or withdrawing feeding tubes is not "medical killing", maintaining them may well produce "involuntary medical living".'[22]

Deepest needs

I tried to make a similar point in my book *New Directions in Moral Theology: The Challenge of Being Human*:

> Some approaches to medical care have so emphasized the preservation of life that they have disregarded the deepest needs of the human person they are supposed to be caring for. Richard McCormick mentions a letter he received claiming that some New York nursing homes were 'concentration camps' and did not let the elderly die with dignity. The writer instanced a 93-year-old senile but physically alert woman who had given up eating and so a feeding tube was inserted against which she fought 'tooth and nail with the most awful expression of fear'. She was then tied to the bed to stop her moving the tube – and for some patients this indignity continues for years! The letter continues: 'It's really a wonderful way of breaking a person's spirit if she has any left at that point.' (*The Critical Calling*, Washington, Georgetown, 1989, p. 386) . . .

> Life may be a foundational good but the other human goods built on its foundation go to make up the quality of life. To fight against the normal dying process when the quality of life has become virtually sub-human is to mistake the place of physical life as a dimension of the good of the human person ... Christian morality is pro-person more than pro-life.[23]

I suspect that our writers would be unhappy with the expression 'mere vegetative life' and would insist that human biological life is an important dimension of personal life and not simply something of utility value to a person. Nevertheless, I feel sure they would keep on insisting that, at least in a life-threatening medical condition, a patient may legitimately weigh up just how good being kept alive in this way is for him or her as a person, all things considered. The U.S. moral theologian, Kevin O'Rourke brings out how wide-ranging the 'all things' to be considered may be.

> A father whose life is threatened because of cancer may decide that his purpose in life would be better fulfilled if he rejected chemotherapy, surgery or hospitalisation in order to devote his time to his family during his remaining days, and to devote his savings toward the education of his children. Given the circumstances, the father is not 'choosing death'. Rather, realizing that he must die sometime, he determines that it is spiritually more beneficial for him to die in the immediate future, rather than to prolong his life for 2, 3 or even 10 years and as a result endanger other values, such as meaningful time with loved ones or the education of his children.[24]

Obviously, this is not arguing in favour of suicide or euthanasia. Neither is it denying the Christian belief that acceptance of unavoidable suffering, evil though such suffering be, can actually be the means of deep spiritual growth. Our Roman Catholic medical ethics tradition has always held firm to this important truth. Nevertheless, it has also insisted that for a person in a life-threatening medical condition the suffering involved in a life sustained by medical intervention need not automatically be presumed to be unavoidable. It is avoidable if the person arrives at a responsible decision that foregoing such medical intervention is, all things considered, more in keeping with respect for their dignity as a human person.

Future possibilities

Traditional medical ethics lays great stress on informed consent as a very important aspect of respect for the dignity of the human person. Nowadays, we refer to this as owning responsibility for our own health. In my parish ministry I am frequently involved with people suffering from cancer who have to make decisions about what kind of treatment will be for their overall good as human persons. That patients are involved in such decisions would warm the heart of the moral theologians whose writings I have been considering.

However, the more we become aware of the human goodness of owning responsibility for our own health, the more we begin to think about future possibilities concerning our health-care. Tragic cases like that of Tony Bland make us realise that, due to a sudden accident or an unexpected heart attack, for instance, we ourselves could end up in a somewhat similar condition. The more medical technology advances, the more we begin to feel anxious lest in future we end up as the 'victims' of misguided treatment decisions. Some people are beginning to be afraid lest they might be subjected to forms of aggressively invasive technological treatment which would extend their lives in a way they would not regard as being beneficial to themselves or others, especially their families. It is this kind of concern which is prompting some people to look at the whole issue of 'advance directives'. These are sometimes referred to – quite inappropriately, to my mind – as 'living wills'. Advance directives are proposed as a way someone can let people know in advance what general forms of medical care would be acceptable to them if they were suddenly placed in a life-threatening situation and were not able to give consent to any medical treatment under consideration. The fact that the Euthanasia Society is also keen on advance directives – though for somewhat different reasons – should not blind us to the fact that, in themselves, advance directives are simply an extension of the notion of informed consent, so precious to the moral theologians we have been considering. I realise, of course, that the advisability of advance directives is a topic very much open to debate and there are substantial arguments put forward both for and against. While acknowledging their moral legitimacy, I am not thereby recommending them as a general procedure.

If I were to write an advance directive to let people know how I would want to be cared for if I came to be in the persistent vegetative state, it might read roughly as follows:

> With regard to artificial respiration and being fed by a nasogastric tube or other similar procedures, I consent to such treatment only as a temporary measure in order to give medical staff time to assess whether there is any realistic hope of my recovering sufficiently to enable me to live a life in which I am able to experience and enjoy the love of my family and friends. However, if and when such a level of recovery is deemed to be impossible, I would like to forego any further use of such treatment and I would want it to be discontinued.

I do not believe that signing such an advance directive would make me a person who is prepared to commit suicide. Nor do I believe I would be instructing those caring for me to kill me. In fact, I believe that signing such an advance directive could be a very responsible Christian decision, in some situations, and fully consistent with the general line of moral reasoning found in traditional Roman Catholic medical ethics. Writing about the decision to make such an advance directive, Richard McCormick remarks: 'It would not necessarily involve a death-aim. It need involve only a thoroughly Christian assertion that there are values greater in life than living, that we all retain the right to decide how we shall live while dying.'[25]

14

Living Positively in a Time of AIDS

A remarkable Ugandan woman, Noerine Kaleeba, who co-founded TASO (The AIDS Support Organisation) after her husband died of AIDS, has coined the phrase, 'living positively with HIV/AIDS'. What that phrase means in practice came home to me a few years ago when I visited Uganda in July 1994 with a CAFOD delegation. There I had the privilege of meeting some wonderful Ugandan women from TASO, all infected with HIV. Their positive attitude to life and the precious opportunity each day presents would put most of us to shame. I had a similar experience a year later in Bangkok and Manila when attending a conference of Asian theologians on HIV/AIDS and visiting various HIV/AIDS projects. In the course of that visit I met some more unforgettable men and women infected with the virus who were challenging examples of living positively with HIV/AIDS. Using fictitious names, let me tell some of their stories.

Maria, one of thirteen children, most of them girls, was raped by her father while still quite young. This crucifying experience left her feeling unclean, worthless and lacking in any sense of self-esteem. In many Asian cultures men expect women to be virgins when they marry, even though they set a much lower standard for themselves. So Maria felt she was now sub-standard. Moreover, young Asian women are usually expected to shoulder the responsibility of looking after their younger sisters and brothers, as well as providing for their parents. In Maria's case she felt this obligation all the more since she wanted to safeguard her young sisters from her father.

To get money to support them, Maria tried a variety of jobs but

---

This is a revised and updated version of my article 'Living with HIV/AIDS', which first appeared in *The Tablet*, 13 May 1995, 597-9.[1]

the pay was never enough. She even suffered further sexual abuse when one employer for whom she was working as a domestic servant attempted to rape her. Eventually she joined the thousands of other girls who, out of desperation and in order to support their families and parents, are forced into prostitution through sheer poverty. For Maria, sadly, this seemed to be the only way to earn enough to support her sisters. She told me she felt so worthless and unclean, she had nothing to lose by becoming a prostitute. It was all she was good for – and it would help to save her sisters from a similar fate. As she was saying this, I could not help thinking of the words of Jesus, 'Greater love has no one than this, to lay down one's life for one's friends.'[2] Almost inevitably Maria soon found herself infected with HIV.

Her HIV-positive status brought her into contact with a Catholic organisation which offered help to people living with HIV/AIDS. They were able to help her out of prostitution and she eventually became involved in their educational work to prevent the spread of the virus. One thing she said to me was, 'When I was told I was HIV-positive, I prayed to God that I might be the last person this would happen to.' She is now also involved with helping to nurse men and women in the more advanced stages of full-blown AIDS. In doing this work she realises that the diminishing effectiveness of her own immune system exposes her to infection. Moreover, she faces daily the suffering and physical degradation that almost certainly lie ahead for her as well. In many cases of full-blown AIDS a person's bodily functions more or less collapse and their condition becomes terrible. Maria spoke very openly to me about the suffering and eventual death that awaited her, probably in the not-too-distant future. She said she trusted God absolutely and knew he would be with her through whatever horrors she had to endure. As she was speaking I was almost moved to tears by her deep faith and utter trust in God.

There is a Christian dictum: hate the sin and love the sinner. That is wise advice as long as we correctly identify what is the sin and who is the sinner. In Maria's case, we could easily interpret that advice as meaning that we should hate Maria's sin of becoming a prostitute but love her, the sinner. I think that would be a serious misreading of Maria's story. One thing that came home to me very forcefully as I listened to Maria and other women with a similar story is that such women should not be branded as sinners. It would be closer to the truth to say that they are victims of sin. They are the victims of the sinful men who abuse them and of the widespread sinful attitude that regards women as inferior to men, a sinful attitude shared by many in the West, even in the Christian Church. They are also victims of the structural sin of an economic system which has destroyed the livelihood of the farming communities from which these women come.

Some people might condemn Maria and say that it is her own fault that she has AIDS. God is punishing her for engaging in prostitution. Those words are more reminiscent of the sentiments of the scribes and Pharisees than of Jesus. I am sure Jesus' reading of Maria's situation would be far more profound. He would take account of the horrendous train of events and of the pressures which eventually drove her into dehumanising prostitution. He would be able to penetrate the depths of her soul and would be deeply moved by her spirit of generous self-sacrifice. 'Greater love has no one ...' Before I left, Maria asked me to pray for her. I replied by asking her to pray for me, and I felt privileged when she promised she would. I honestly believe that her prayers will carry greater weight before the Lord than mine.

Wimple, Thaksin and Samphan are all men who have become HIV-positive through contact with prostitutes. In contemporary Thai culture it is quite common for married men to frequent prostitutes, though these same men demand much stricter standards of their own women both before and within marriage. As soon as it was known that Wimol, Thaksin and Samphan were HIV-positive, they began to suffer the stigma that people living with HIV/AIDS experience. All three of them were rejected and disowned by their families and friends. They lost their jobs and became unemployable. Their health went to pieces and, destitute, they ended up in the only hospital which offered free treatment to people living with HIV/AIDS.

Eventually each of them found himself transferred from this hospital to a Catholic AIDS hospice with the expectation that they would soon die there. In fact, at this stage they were probably dying of neglect rather than full-blown AIDS. Given loving and compassionate care and good nourishment in the hospice, all three of them have recovered for the time being. Each of them is dedicating his life to working in Church-related projects concerned with HIV/AIDS' prevention and education, as well as caring for HIV-positive men and women who, like themselves, have been abandoned by those closest to them. Once again, the dedication of all of them is heroic and the depth of their faith commitment is remarkable. On their own admission, the quality of their lives has been deepened enormously. Wimol actually said to me, 'AIDS is my gift', and Thaksin told the assembled theologians at our meeting, 'To compare my life before HIV/AIDS and my life today, is like comparing night and day'.

All three of these men have experienced profound healing – not of the virus but of that attitude and lifestyle which led to their infection and which subsequently made them a health hazard to others. Today, far from being a health hazard, they are safeguarding other people's health by their HIV/AIDS prevention educational work.

Cleo is a woman whose husband died of AIDS, as did two of her five children. Being a drug-user as well as sleeping around with other women, he may have become infected by either activity. In any case, he has passed the virus on to Cleo and through her to their two children born subsequent to her becoming HIV-positive. Cleo now spends much of her time sharing her own personal story with other people as part of an educational project to counteract the terrible fear of people who are HIV-positive and the discrimination against them which is widespread in Thai society. The rest of her time is devoted to helping promote and sustain a family atmosphere in a drop-in centre and temporary residence where she lives with a group of men and women who are all HIV-positive or with full-blown AIDS.

Like the others I have mentioned, Cleo's deep faith and trust in God was tangible. A woman who had experienced great poverty and hardship in the agricultural north of the country and who had been denied the benefit of a proper education, here she was addressing an assembly of theologians from all over Asia! The impact of her words on everyone was enormous and was to play an important part in our deliberations for the rest of the week. I think we all interpreted the experience as God speaking to us through Cleo.

The morning after I returned from my visit to Asia, the Sunday Gospel faced me with the words: 'Blessed are you poor; the kingdom of God is yours'.[3] My mind went immediately to those whose stories I have told above. I could imagine Jesus saying to Maria, Wimol, Thaksin, Samphan and Cleo: 'Blessed are you, who are living with HIV/AIDS.' Jesus welcomed and ate with people whom the so-called righteous of his day condemned as sinners and religiously unclean. Society may have rejected you, Jesus told them, but I am showing you that you are especially precious in the eyes of God. I am sure that is the message he would want Maria and her companions to hear from his followers.

I do not in any way want to romanticise HIV/AIDS or imply that it is anything other than a deadly viral infection. AIDS brings death as a result of one of a number of opportunistic diseases whose symptoms, for the most part, cause terrible suffering, as well as being degrading and disintegrating to the human person. Its rapid spread, especially in the developing countries through heterosexual intercourse, is a human tragedy on a colossal scale. Huge numbers are already HIV-positive and the projections for the near future are frightening.

A report in *The Guardian* states that 'more than 30 million people – one in 100 sexually active adults worldwide – are now living with HIV, and 16,000 more become infected with the virus each day, according to the United Nations.' The report continues:

> In an alarming report, published yesterday, the UN admitted that it had "grossly underestimated the scale of the global AIDS epidemic. A leap from 22.6 million people in 1996 partly reflects a more accurate method of collecting data . . ." 'The more we know about the AIDS epidemic, the worse it appears to be,' Dr Peter Piot, executive director of the UN programme said. "If current transmission rates hold steady,

> by the year 2000 the number of people living with HIV or AIDS will soar to 40 million." The report said 5.8 million people were projected to become infected with HIV in 1997, compared with an estimated 5.3 million in 1996 – far more than the 3.1 million that doctors had originally estimated... "The main message of our report is that the AIDS epidemic is far from over. In fact, it's far, far worse," Dr Piot said.
>
> The new figures show the number of people thought to be living with HIV or AIDS includes 20.6 million in sub-Saharan Africa, 6 million in south and south-east Asia, 1.3 million in Latin America and 530,000 in western Europe. By far the worst-hit region is sub-Saharan Africa, where 7.4% of all people aged 15 to 49 are thought to be carrying HIV. The South African government estimates 2.4 million of its citizens have HIV, while in Botswana, the number of HIV-infected people has doubled in five years, standing at 25 to 30% of the entire adult population.[4]

The pandemic in South and South-east Asia may be growing at a pace reminiscent of sub-Saharan Africa in the early 1980s and its potential to become widespread is even greater, given an adult population of nearly 500 million as compared with 225 million in sub-Saharan Africa. Between early 1992 and mid-1994 the estimate for HIV infections in South and South-east Asia rose from just over 1 million to 2.5 million. As the above report from *The Guardian* makes clear, that figure has now nearly tripled to 6 million in only three years! The Asian countries worst affected seem to be India and Thailand. If no major changes occur, by the year 2000 there may be a cumulative total of between two to four million HIV infections in Thailand alone.

Noerine Kaleeba's slogan 'living positively with HIV/AIDS' implies that every effort must be made to find a medical cure and one which, unlike the present combination therapies, does more than buy extra time for those affected. It is equally important that it be a cure which is economically available to the vast numbers of poor who are affected by HIV/AIDS in the developing world.

Moreover, Noerine's slogan does not just apply to people who are infected with HIV. It applies to all of us. A few years ago some people at a conference in the Vatican were shocked at a banner which read: 'The Body of Christ has AIDS'. Yet the truth of that statement can be defended theologically. Moreover, it is equally true that the human family, God's family, has AIDS. This truth must have an impact on how all of us in the human family lives our lives. We are all faced with the challenge of 'living positively with HIV/AIDS'.

At the end of the consultation in Bangkok, our assembly of Asian theologians was in agreement that so enormous is the threat of HIV/AIDS to the human family (and especially to the poor in the developing countries) that it can rightly be said that we are living in a 'time of HIV/AIDS', to borrow a phrase from the Irish theologian, Enda McDonagh. By 'time' here is meant the biblical notion of *kairos*, a precious time of opportunity which must not be squandered. Of course, the Asian theologians were not suggesting that HIV/AIDS is a plague sent by God to punish human sin and make us mend our ways. Such a suggestion would be blasphemous. Nevertheless, when the pandemic is subjected to social analysis, it becomes clear that some of the more fundamental underlying causes for its rapid spread are to be found in the 'sinful structures' which undergird the global life of our human family. One of these is the structural poverty within which many developing countries are imprisoned and which seems to be causally linked to the prosperity of the West, especially those benefiting most from it and the élite minorities in developing countries working in collusion with them. The other is the implicit denial of the full and equal dignity of women which can render dysfunctional so many dimensions of social, cultural and family life. Though this may perhaps be experienced to a lesser extent by women in the West, the form this structural injustice takes in many developing countries and in their cultures has grave implications for the lives of women, especially poor women in society.

These two 'sinful structures' are very closely interconnected. An example of this interconnection can be seen in the various ways they combine together to expose women in the developing countries to the threat of HIV/AIDS. Thus many women become infected with the HIV virus simply through being faithful to their husbands, who either follow a double standard of morality or whose employment forces them to be away from home for long periods. Poverty and the inferior status imposed on women force many of them (including young girls) into the sex industry which, linked to sex tourism, is itself seen as an economic measure to help some developing countries climb out of poverty. Poverty and AIDS are also connected in that drugs crops are often the only means the poor have to earn a meagre living and the drugs trade is often bound up with the sex industry. Further, low-quality medical care can sometimes result in HIV-infected blood being used in transfusions which poses a particular danger to women who have a greater need for them because of frequent pregnancies. Finally, female genital mutilation and a variety of other cultural practices, including wife inheritance, create 'HIV-friendly' conditions which leave women more vulnerable to HIV infection. Such practices, especially female genital mutilation, affect millions of women:

> At the end of her novel, *Possessing the Secret of Joy* (London, Vintage, 1993), Alice Walker mentions that it is estimated that "from ninety to one hundred million women and girls living today in African, Far Eastern and Middle Eastern countries have been genitally mutilated." (p. 266) I am told that female genital mutilation as practised in some parts of Africa yields a total of ten million new cases of mutilation each year! This practice leaves women, especially young women, more at risk of HIV infection due to a number of reasons, the main one being the fact that it leaves them with permanent scar tissues which are open to abrasions in the course of sexual activity.[5]

The rapid spread of HIV/AIDS in developing countries can certainly in part be attributed to irresponsible sexual behaviour by some of those who have been infected with the virus. But that explanation overlooks the question: who bears primary responsibility for this sexual behaviour? Is it women like Maria, driven through poverty into prostitution as the only way to support their families? Is it young husbands forced to spend most of the year in an all-male dormitory away from their wives and families in order to hold down a poorly-paid job in some distant mine or building site? Market forces exert real force on people's lives. They can be a form of violence. Unless market forces are restrained and regulated by social considerations, the end result can be a drastic reduction in the effective freedom of the poorest in our world. The poor majority of our world, especially in the developing countries, are increasingly paying the cost of the prosperity of the wealthy minority. And one major item in the present cost is the rapid spread of HIV/AIDS in their midst. A challenging statement in n. 2269 of *The Catechism of the Catholic Church* might be relevant here: 'Those whose usurious and avaricious dealings lead to the hunger and death of their brethren in the human family indirectly commit homicide, which is imputable to them.' Those are strong words.

In the final analysis, it is fair to ask: whose irresponsibility lies at the root of much of the sexual behaviour which is assisting the spread of HIV/AIDS? Do we limit our search for the answer to that question to the behaviour of the poor of the developing countries or do we also need to look nearer home to the behaviour of the prosperous élite here in the West? Heroic and inspiring work is being done in some of the developing countries to promote behavioural change among sexually-active young people. Perhaps even more important is the need for behavioural change in the developed world – in economic rather than sexual behaviour.

Noerine Kaleeba insists that we must all live positively with HIV/AIDS. Those of us who are Christians need to ask ourselves where we stand before such a challenge. Are we and our churches living positively with HIV/AIDS? The answer is, probably, yes and no.

Yes, in the sense that many committed Christians are responding to the HIV/AIDS pandemic with tremendous generosity and self-sacrifice. I saw plenty of evidence of that on my visits to Uganda, Thailand and the Philippines. And I know many Christians are equally committed here in the West. Yes, too, in that many statements from different Churches have called for care and compassion for people living with HIV/AIDS and have strongly rejected any suggestion that the virus has been sent as a punishment from God.

Nevertheless, perhaps some of the answer is 'no'. For instance, maybe our Churches are not giving the high priority they should to promoting the full and equal dignity of women and to combating whatever violates this in the attitudes, structures and behaviour found in society and especially within the Churches themselves. It is possible, too, that, particularly in the case of the Roman Catholic Church, some aspects of our teaching on sexual ethics are part of the problem rather than helping to provide a solution. Time and again I found the credibility of the Catholic Church in this field compromised by the absoluteness and intransigence of its stance on contraception and the translation of this stance by some bishops into outright opposition to any Government programmes involving the promotion of condoms as one strategy among many in their education and prevention policies. This was said to me not just by those hostile to the Church but frequently by utterly committed Catholics deeply involved at a practical level in the field of HIV/AIDS. I also found many people dissatisfied with the current Church teaching on homosexuality and convinced that a more positive stance is needed to do justice to the experience of deeply committed homosexual relationships and their self-sacrificing love, faithfulness and generosity in the face of the ravages of HIV/AIDS. The Christian Churches have a most serious responsibility to make sure that their teaching on sexual ethics does not impose burdens on men and women which would, in practice, oblige them to live negatively rather than positively with HIV/AIDS.

Paradoxically, 'living positively with HIV/AIDS' could offer our contemporary world a healthier lifestyle. If our human family is open to the opportunity offered in this 'time of AIDS', we will move forward on three key fronts: we will take effective steps to secure economic justice for all; we will eliminate whatever contradicts the full and equal dignity of women; and we will formulate a more satisfactory person-respecting sexual ethic. I firmly believe that for all of us today 'living positively with HIV/AIDS' is an integral element of the message of the gospel.

Notes

Introduction

1. *Bioethics and Belief* (London: Sheed & Ward, 1984), p. 112.
2. Chelmsford: Matthew James Publishing Ltd, 1995.
3. Dublin: Veritas, 1996, p. 7.
4. Yves Congar, Hans Küng and Daniel O'Hanlon (eds.), *Council Speeches of Vatican II* (London: Sheed & Ward, 1964), p. 51.
5. For further reading, see Kevin T. Kelly, *New Directions in Sexual Ethics: Moral Theology and the Challenge of AIDS* (London: Geoffrey Chapman, 1998), especially pp. 174–6.
6. London: G. Chapman, 1994.
7. *God in South Africa* (London: Catholic Institute for International Relations, 1988).
8. *The Critical Calling* (Washington: Georgetown University Press, 1989), p. 385.
9. 'A Medical Dilemma' in *The Month*, 1993, 138–44, and 'Rest for Tony Bland' in *The Tablet*, 13 March 1993, 332–5.
10. *The Tablet*, 1 King Street Cloisters, Clifton Walk, London W6 0QZ; *The Month*, 114 Mount Street, London W1Y 6AH; *The Way/The Way Supplement*, Heythrop College, Kensington Square, London W8 5HQ; , *Priests and People*, Blackfriars, Buckingham Road, Cambridge CB3 0DD; *New Blackfriars*, Blackfriars, Oxford OX1 3LY.

Chapter 1: From Vatican II into the Millennium: Blueprint for a Contemporary Parish

1. Vatican edition, p. 6.
2. *With Hope in Our Hearts* (London: Hodder & Stoughton, 1994).

Chapter 2: Struggling to Live the Gospel in Inner-city Liverpool: a Case Study

1. A very moving, though harrowing, description of the impact of the Irish Famine years on this area of Liverpool was given by Professor Frank Neal of Salford University in a lecture, entitled 'Liverpool, the Cemetery of Ireland', at a special Great Hunger Memorial Service held on 3 October 1997 in St Anthony's, Scotland Road (the 'mother church' of the area) in the presence of Archbishop Kelly of Liverpool. The text of this lecture is printed in *The Great Hunger Commemoration Service* which can be purchased from Fr Tom Williams, St Anthony's, Scotland Road, Liverpool L3 5BD, price £5.00. It is a resumè of Neal's more extensive research published in his book, *Black '47: Britain and the Famine Irish* (London: Macmillan, 1998).
2. Cf. Chapter 1.

Chapter 3: Collaborative Ministry: a Pastoral Experience in Skelmersdale

1. pp. 30 and 19.
2. A few years before this mission statement was composed, one of the earlier

priest members of the team, Fr Michael McKenna, initiated a major youth employment scheme in Skelmersdale called 'Tomorrow's People Today' (TPT). True to the principles of collaborative ministry, it was largely staffed and directed by local people. That probably accounts for the remarkable fact that it has survived the many changes in Government policy over the years. Today, more than twenty years later, TPT is still helping young people in Skelmersdale to develop confidence in themselves through good work experience and skills-training.

Chapter 5: Collaborative Ministry in the Exercise of Teaching Authority

1. cf. *Lumen Gentium*, n. 12.
2. cf. *The Theology of Vatican II* (London, 1967), p. 36.
3. cf. *Gaudium et Spes*, n. 44.
4. cf. also Decree on Ecumenism, n. 3.
5. William Abbott (ed.), *The Documents of Vatican II* (London: Geoffrey Chapman, 1966), p. 226.
6. cf. *Gaudium et Spes*, nn. 44 and 58.
7. In *New Directions* in *Sexual Ethics: Moral Theology and the Challenge of AIDS* (London: Geoffrey Chapman, 1998), pp. 96–9, I have suggested that it can sometimes be helpful to interpret some authoritative teaching statements on specific ethical issues as important contributions to an ongoing conversation.

Chapter 6: Co-responsibility and Accountability within a Sinful Church

1. Karl Rahner, *Theological Investigations* (London: Darton, Longman & Todd, 1969), vol. 6, chs. 17 and 18.
2. Luke 18:9–14.
3. John 8:3–11.
4. *Catholic International*, vol. 3, no. 19, 936.
5. Quoted in Bernard Häring, *My Witness for the Church* (New York: Paulist Press), p. 227.
6. ibid.
7. ibid., p. 90.
8. cf. *Briefing*, 28 April 1994, 8.
9. *Origins*, 16 October 1997, 301–5.
10. cf. *The Tablet*, 8 November 1997, 1447.
11. cf. *The Tablet*, 6 December 1997, 1555.
12. cf. *The Tablet*, 17 October 1992, 1309.

Chapter 7: Moral Theology and Pastoral Care in the Parish

1. Matt. 13:24–30.
2. *Summa contra Gentiles*, III, 133.
3. *The Tablet*, 3 August 1991, 935–7.
4. Jack Mahoney, 'Moral Reasoning in Medical Ethics', in *The Month*, 1963, 294. I have written further on this topic in Chapter 4 ('In the light of experience: morality and change') in *New Directions in Moral Theology: The Challenge of Being Human* (London: Geoffrey Chapman, 1992).

Chapter 8: The Changing Face of Moral Theology

1. Following the eight-dimension analysis of Professor Louis Janssens of Louvain, I have tried to fill out what this means in Chapter 3 of my *New Directions in Moral Theology: The Challenge of Being Human* (London: Geoffrey Chapman, 1992).
2. In *New Directions in Sexual Ethics: Moral Theology and the Challenge of AIDS* (London: Geoffrey Chapman, 1998) I have looked at some issues in the field of sexual ethics in the light of the Vatican II criterion of the good of the

human person, integrally and adequately considered.
3. London: Collins, 1987, chapter 5.
4. cf. my *Conscience: Dictator or Guide? A Study in 17th century Protestant Moral Theology* (London: Geoffrey Chapman, 1967).
5. Kevin Nichols, *Refracting the Truth: Learning the Languages of Faith* (Dublin: Lindisfarne Books, 1997), p. 39.
6. *Bioethics and Belief* (London: Sheed & Ward, 1984), p. 112.
7. I have tried to develop this line of thought further in Chapter 2 of *New Directions in Sexual Ethics: Moral Theology and the Challenge of AIDS* (London: Geoffrey Chapman, 1998).
8. *The Making of Moral Theology* (Oxford: OUP, 1987), p. 295.
9. *Economic Justice for All: Catholic Social Teaching and the U.S. Economy*, full text in *Origins*, 27 November 1986, 408–55.
10. 'How Bishops and Theologians Relate', June 1986 address at Marquette University, full text in *Origins*, 31 July 1986, 169–74 (at 174).
11. 'Notes on Moral Theology, 1986' in *Theological Studies*, 1987, 87–105 (at 102).
12. *Theological Investigations*, vol. XIV (London, Darton, Longman & Todd, 1976), p. 94.
13. I wrestle with this issue in *New Directions in Sexual Ethics: Moral Theology and the Challenge of AIDS*; cf. also Chapter 14.

Chapter 9: Life in Christ: The Moral Teaching of the Catechism of the Catholic Church

1. Text in *The Ecumenical Review*, 1996, 143–54.

Chapter 10: Conscience Formation and Consciousness-raising in the Parish

1. *Summa Theologiae*, I–II, 106, 1.
2. cf. *Summa contra Gentiles*, III, n. 122.
3. London: Geoffrey Chapman, 1998, pp. 12–13.

Chapter 11: Saints or Sinners? Towards a Spirituality of Growth Out of Sin

1. Matthew 9:13.
2. Another attempt to grapple with the topic of sin in a way which might be pastorally helpful at a practical level is found in 'The inhumanity of sin and the humanity of forgiveness' which is chapter 7 in my *New Directions in Moral Theology: The Challenge of Being Human* (London: Geoffrey Chapman, 1992).
3. 'The Power of Anger in the Work of Love', in Carol Robb (ed.), *Making the Connections: Essays in Feminist Social Ethics* (Boston: Beacon Press, 1985), pp. 11–12.
4. cf. *The Church in the World of Today*, n. 26.
5. cf. *The Church in the World of Today*, nn. 4–10.
6. 'Theological Trends: Sin and Sacramental Reconciliation, I. Contemporary Reflection on Sin', in *The Way*, 1984, 221–2.
7. John 8:7.
8. Full report in Milwaukee *Catholic Herald*, 24 May 1990.
9. *Summa contra Gentiles*, III, c. 133 – my own paraphrase.
10. *God in South Africa* (London: Catholic Institute for International Relations, 1988), p. 38.
11. ibid.
12. ibid., p. 49.
13. ibid., p. 57.
14. In *Studia Moralia*, 1988, pp. 61–100.
15. ibid., 92.
16. ibid., 92–3.

17. ibid., 93.
18. ibid., 94.
19. ibid., 94.
20. ibid., 88.
21. ibid., 96.
22. ibid., 96.
23. 'Latin America: Place of Sin and Place of Forgiveness', in *Concilium n. 184 – Special Issue on Forgiveness*, 45–56, at 46.
24. ibid., 48.
25. ibid., 48–9.
26. John 10:10.

Chapter 12: Embryo Research and the Dignity of the Human Person

1. Cambridge University Press, 1988.
2. London: Sheed & Ward, 1984, p. 78.
3. cf. 'The animation tradition in the light of contemporary philosophy', in G.R. Dunstan and Mary J. Seller (eds.), *The Status of the Human Embryo* (Oxford University Press/King Edward's Hospital Fund for London, 1989), p. 100.
4. cf. *Warnock Report*, nn. 11.25–11.29.

Chapter 13: Prolonging Life Unduly or Letting Die: Christian Morality – Pro-life or Pro-person

1. Gerald Kelly, *Medico-Moral Problems* (Dublin: Clonmore and Reynolds, 1960).
2. Edwin Healy, *Medical Ethics* (Chicago: Loyola University Press, 1956).
3. Kelly, *Medico–Moral Problems*, p. 129.
4. cf. John J. Paris, 'The Catholic Tradition on the Use of Nutrition and Fluids', in Kevin M. Wildes, Francesc Abel and John C. Harvey (eds.), *Birth, Suffering and Death: Catholic Perspectives at the Edges of Life* (Dordrecht, The Netherlands: Kluwer Academic Publishers, 1992), pp. 189–208, at p. 202.
5. Kelly, *Medico–Moral Problems*, p. 139.
6. ibid., p. 136.
7. ibid., p. 137.
8. Healy, p. 69.
9. In *Irish Ecclesiastical Record*, 1941, 552–4.
10. Gerald Kelly, 'The duty of using artificial means of preserving life' in *Theological Studies*, 1950, 217.
11. cf. full text of Pius XII's statement in Kevin M. Wildes *et al.* (eds.), pp. 209–15, at p. 212.
12. London: G. Chapman, 1994.
13. 'The A.M.A. statement on tube-feeding: an ethical analysis' in *America*, 22 November 1986, 321–3, at 322.
14. ' On Withdrawing Artificial Nutrition and Hydration' in *Origins*, 7 June 1990, 53–5, at 54.
15. Sheila Cassidy, 'Care of the dying' in *The Tablet*, 3 April 1993, p. 431.
16. Thomas A. Shannon and James J. Walter, 'The PVS Patient and the Forgoing/Withdrawing of Medical Nutrition and Hydration' in James J. Walter and Thomas A. Shannon (eds.), *Quality of Life: the New Medical Dilemma* (New Jersey: Paulist Press, 1990), p. 211.
17. 'The Duty to Preserve Life', in *Theological Studies*, 1951, 550–6, at 554.
18. Richard McCormick, *The Critical Calling* (Washington: Georgetown University Press, 1989), p. 385.
19. John J. Paris, 'The Catholic Tradition on the Use of Nutrition and Fluids' in Kevin M. Wildes *et al.* (eds.), pp. 189–208, at p. 206.
20. Quoted by Paul Schotsmans in 'When the Dying Person Looks Me in the Face: An Ethics of Responsibility for Dealing with the Problem of the Patient in a

Persistently Vegetative State' in Wildes *et al* (eds.), pp.127–143 at p. 140.
21. *Quality of Life*, p. 214.
22. ibid., p. 220.
23. London: Geoffrey Chapman, 1992.
24. 'The A.M.A. statement on tube-feeding: an ethical analysis' in *America*, 22 November 1986, pp. 321–3, at p. 323.
25. *The Critical Calling*, p. 382.

Chapter 14: Living Positively in a Time of AIDS

1 I have written at greater length on this same topic in my *New Directions in Sexual Ethics: Moral Theology and the Challenge of AIDS* (London: Geoffrey Chapman, 1998). Cf. also my article 'The Challenge of AIDS', in *Spirituality and Ethics: The Way Supplement*, 1997/8, 46–54.
2. John 15:13.
3. Matthew 5:3.
4. *The Guardian*, 17 November 1997.
5. *New Directions in Sexual Ethics: Moral Theology and the Challenge of AIDS*, p. 7.

Index